GOSPEL-CENTERED
LEADERSHIP
Becoming the servant God wants you to be

by Steve Timmis

Gospel-centered leadership
© 2012 Steve Timmis/The Good Book Company
All rights reserved.

The Good Book Company (USA)
170 W. Main St, Purcellville VA, 20132
Tel: 866 244 2165; International: +1 866 244 2165
Email: sales@thegoodbook.com

The Good Book Company
Blenheim House, 1 Blenheim Road, Epsom, Surrey KT19 9AP, UK
Tel: 0333-123-0880; International: +44 (0) 208 942 0880
Email: admin@thegoodbook.co.uk

Websites:
North America: www.thegoodbook.com
UK: www.thegoodbook.co.uk
Australia: www.thegoodbook.com.au
New Zealand: www.thegoodbook.co.nz

Scripture quotations are from The Holy Bible, New International Version, Copyright © 1973,
1978, 1984, 2011 by Biblica, Inc.™ Used by permission. All rights reserved worldwide.

ISBN: 9781908317834

Cover design: Steve Devane
Printed in China through Asia Pacific Offset Limited

CONTENTS

INTRODUCTION

Having been a Christian since the tender age of 10 years old, I consider myself well acquainted with leadership in all sorts of shapes and sizes. Some of it good, some of it bad, and some of it just plain ugly.

I have seen trained leaders lead badly and untrained ones lead with skill and sensitivity. I have also seen lay leaders make a compelling case for formal training simply by their incompetence. I have seen gifted leaders lead effortlessly and others in positions of leadership carry it like a heavy burden.

This variety of experience has convinced me that leadership is a given. It is one of those things that just is! In any group of any size, a leader will emerge. Someone who takes initiative, assumes responsibility for the activity and direction of that group. Someone who thinks they know best and that it won't be too long before everyone else agrees with them!

I have also read countless books on leadership and gleaned helpful insights from leaders, both male and female, in the worlds of commerce, industry, politics and sport.

All of this exposure to leadership over so many years will have inevitably influenced and even shaped my attitude to, opinion of, thoughts on and practice of the art of leadership. I have seen leaders I want to emulate and other leaders and leadership styles that I abhor.

But in the end, I have a deep and enduring conviction that it is the gospel that should shape my attitude to and practice of leadership. That what God has done in Christ should define who I am as a leader and for what kind of leader I am. That there should be something distinctive about leadership among the people of God, that springs from the message that brings it into being.

In the person of Jesus Christ, we have a unique and compelling model of leadership and the supreme example of authentic and effective leadership. All leaders who claim to be Christian should want to lead like him and be a leader like him. To love like he loves, serve like he serves, be wise as he is wise, and lead so that others follow willingly, eagerly and safely.

But I also know my heart—that it is deceitful and wicked, full of pride and self-promotion. I know that my leadership can easily become "all about me". So gospel-centered leadership must, in the first instance, lead from a position of repentance and faith. The gospel calls me to lead by example, and that is primarily in the recognition of my deep and enduring need for Jesus and the patient work of his indwelling Spirit.

The leadership style of someone who has been gripped by the gospel and captured by Christ will be profoundly different from that of someone who labors under delusions of their own adequacy.

The aim of this book is to help us think through what shape, color and texture the gospel gives to leadership. It is for leaders—formal or informal, experienced or novice, actual or aspiring, skilled or simply doing the best they can. It is for leaders of churches, small groups, youth groups, large groups and tiny groups of one or two.

My willingness to become a leader in a church context was in no small part because of my experience of leadership. I want to put on record my deep appreciation of those leaders who shaped me as a young boy and adolescent—Rod Townsend, Ron Price and Pete Bellingham. I am thankful to the Lord for the way he used them to develop me, and for the men they all were.

But in the end, it is the Savior by his Spirit through his Word who constantly calls me back to himself and gives me a desire and ability to lead among his people, conscious that he is the Shepherd and not only do "they" remain his sheep, but I am always one also.

Finding your way around

Consider this

A scenario—often based on a real-life situation—which raises some kind of dilemma or frustration in gospel ministry.

Biblical background

A relevant Bible passage together with some questions to help you think it through.

Read all about it

A discussion of the principle, both in terms of its theological underpinning and its contemporary application.

Questions for discussion

Questions that can be used for group discussion or personal reflection.

Ideas for action

Some ideas or an exercise to help people think through the application of the principle to their own situation.

We have tried to make this book work:

- whether it is read by an individual or used as the basis for group discussion.

- whether you want to work through it systematically or turn to particular topics as they arise in church life.

PART ONE
PRINCIPLES

Gospel-centered leadership

1 GOD RULES! OK?

Principle

The people of God belong to God.

 Consider this

Paul took a deep breath and counted to ten. There was no other way to put it: sometimes people were just a pain in the neck.

He found it so frustrating when he could see what they were doing wrong. But they just kept on doing it no matter what he said to them. Sometimes dictatorship seemed an attractive option…

He had the experience, gifting and track record to equip him for this job; if they had anything about them they would see that.

Herding sheep was easy—this was more like herding cats.

Biblical background

Read Genesis 2 – 3

❓ What freedom does God give the man in 2 v 16?

❓ What boundaries does God set on this freedom and why (2 v 17)?

❓ What makes crossing this boundary attractive to Eve in 3v 4-6?

❓ What are the results of Adam and Eve's rebellion (3 v 10-19)?

❓ The serpent suggests that God is being deceitfully restrictive in the boundary that He set (3 v 4-5). Was He?

Read all about it

I first became aware of the defining influence of culture in the former Soviet Union, through the issue of leadership. The Soviet Union of the late 1980s was a vast empire held together by the ruthless totalitarian regime that Stalin had created. It was interesting to observe Soviet church leadership in that context—particularly in those churches most viciously harassed by the state.

People in these churches had faced great suffering because of their loyalty to the Lord Jesus. They were led by men of courage and conviction. Yet the leadership of the pastor often reflected the auto-cratic style of leadership in the wider culture—church leaders could see no other way to lead.

This should get us thinking. Unlike the former Soviet Union, the western world is sold on the notion of democracy—at least as an ideal. It is taken for granted that democracy is the best (maybe even the only legitimate) form of government. This default towards democracy permeates every area of life, creating two issues:

1. In an established democratic culture, "my" opinion is as valid as any other opinion. I have a right for my voice to be heard and for my views to be expressed and given due weight.
2. In a representative democracy (such as the USA or the UK) individuals are elected to a governing body to act on behalf of the people. In this system, someone can be elected and then quickly replaced by someone else if they no longer enjoy the favor of the people. Elected leaders are often not respected, and their position is often viewed with cynicism.

Leadership is always going to be contentious in such a world.

There is a recognition of the necessity and value of leadership along with a dislike of "being told what to do" and a rejection of forms of respect and deference to those in power. Acknowledging our culture's view of leadership is important because it alerts us to at least some of the issues that shape us. We are always in danger of resorting to a prevailing cultural model or mind-set.

It would be naïve to claim that we can (or should) rid ourselves of all cultural influences. However, because we instinctively reflect our culture, we should do all we can to ensure that our understanding of and response to leadership is shaped by the Bible rather than our culture.

Who rules?

But leadership isn't a problem for us simply because of cultural attitudes. Genesis 3 shows that rebellion and grasping for autonomy—self rule—is a central part of human nature. Essentially, we all want to be "god" of our own worlds—we all want to lead ourselves.

The Bible begins with a clear assertion that this is God's world. He made it. He rules it. He made the first man and woman, and he rules them. The events narrated in Genesis 2 *assume* God's right to set boundaries on human freedom. Genesis 3 *demonstrates* that right, along with the rest of the Bible.

Throughout the whole tragic and glorious story from Genesis to Revelation, God's right of rule is asserted. His rule extends over all creation and the whole of history. It includes his people, but is not limited to them.

History, as the Bible understands it, is not the product of chance. History really is *His-story* because it is the result of his design and purposes; it's an expression of God's sovereign will. History is the context in which God rules, and judgment and grace are the defining qualities of his loving rule.

God is the Leader

None of the forms of human leadership which emerge in Bible history undermine this fundamental truth. We see God's rule exercised in the fine and precise details of his judgments passed on Adam and Eve, Cain, the human race in the flood, and the insurrection at Babel. We see his rule exercised in the grace extended to Eve in bearing children, the protection of Cain, the confusion of languages at Babel and his choice of Abram to be the means through which the rebellious nations will be blessed.

God's "macro rule" is seen in his calling of nations such as Assyria and Babylon to be the sword of his judgment against his people. It is also shown in his judgment on those nations for their failure to honor God and acknowledge him as King. his "micro rule" is seen in the lives of characters such as Joseph, Moses and Ruth. At one and the same time, God interweaves his great purposes with the fine detail as his purposes for the world and individuals are fulfilled.

This is seen supremely in Christ. The phrase *"fullness of time"* (Gal 4 v 4) shows that Jesus' arrival in human history was a fixed moment in the purposes of God. When Jesus began his public ministry, he did so with the declaration that "the time is fulfilled" (Mark 1 v 14). In other words, the moment has arrived—the decreed time is here. In his Pentecost sermon, Peter articulated this God-driven view of history when he said boldly: "This Man, delivered over by the predetermined plan and foreknowledge of God, you nailed to a cross by the hands of godless men." (Acts 2 v 23)

Finally, the book of Revelation shows—through the images of the seals, trumpets and bowls—that history in all of its apparent chaos and conflict is nonetheless directed from the throne room of heaven. From there, the Lion of Judah, who is the slain Lamb, unfolds a pre-ordained plan as history moves inexorably towards the return of the King.

We must keep these broad truths about God's total rule in mind when we think about the concept and practicalities of leadership. I remember the story of a new minister who announced his arrival at the church's Annual General Meeting by saying:

> "We need to remember that this church is not a democracy, a plutocracy, an aristocracy, a monarchy or a bureaucracy. It is a theocracy. And my name is Theo!"

Hopefully, no church leader would be quite so crass in describing or thinking of their role! But it is surprising how often such an attitude lurks beneath the surface, coming out in various ways and times. When leaders are well respected, the church can give up too much authority to them—they, in turn, can be all too ready to accept it. Dictatorship is still dictatorship, even when it's benign. On the other hand, when the flock is rebellious and stubborn, power can be grasped and authority asserted by the pastor out of nothing more noble than frustration.

And it's not just the pastor problem. Such an attitude can lurk in the heart of all kinds of leaders in the local church. A Bible-study group leader who dominates the conversation, and crushes dissent. An elder who schemes behind the scenes to assert their control. A church administrator who uses their privileges to dominate the way things are done. The root of many of these misuses of power lies in a simple failure to believe Lesson One in the Bible.

God rules!

What we are now as the church is meant to model and point to the future of Jesus' direct rule. Any biblical theology of leadership must look at the period of time known as the "not yet" or "still to come". We look forward to a time that will take us beyond the opening chapters of Revelation to the great vision at the end (chapters 21 – 22). Here, the Lamb rules his people not from the distance of heaven, but from among us, as we rule over his new creation and enjoy life as it was meant to be lived.

So, leadership is important, but it must be leadership that gives expression to the continuing leadership of King Jesus over his people. True leadership does that in two ways:

1. Faithfully expounding God's word so that it is God's voice that is heard;

2. Conforming to the servant-hearted, cross-shaped leadership of Jesus Himself.

God rules his world—God rules his people. He has never and will never abdicate. This simple truth, simply stated, should be a source of great joy to those who lead God's people. It means that our role as leaders is specific and our responsibility limited. We are set free to do what we are called to do, confident that God will do what he will do. Praise God that the people of God are precisely that—the people of God!

God rules. Ok?

You bet it is!

Questions for reflection

❓ What kinds of churches have you been part of? How has the leadership been viewed in them?

❓ Who is your ideal leader? Think of a hero you admire in politics, history and church life. What was their style, and why do you find it attractive?

❓ What style of leadership do you think you currently exercise?
- I am in charge—do what I say (dictator)
- I am the slave and servant of the people who have elected or hired me to be their leader
- I am not in control at all (anarchy!)
- I am technically in control, but I have to jump through endless hoops in order to get anything done (bureaucracy)

❓ Which kind of leader would you prefer to be?

❓ What frustrates you most about your leadership role?

❓ What is your greatest fear in leadership?

❓ Can you see some ways that your views of leadership or authority are shaped by your culture? If you cannot, ask a friend who is not from your culture—they are sure to see some!

❓ What comes to mind when you hear the word "leadership"? Are your impressions mostly positive or mostly negative? Why is that?

❓ Think of some ways in which a leader will do the wrong things if they forget that God is the one who is truly in control. Which of these are you most tempted to fall for?

Gospel-centered leadership

2 EXAMPLES AND (BROKEN) MODELS

Principle

God rules through his servants

Consider this

Adam was enjoying the book on leadership his parents had given him for Christmas. The author made a lot of sense and his experience spoke for itself. Although Adam knew that he would never be a leader of that caliber, he was certain there were things that he could learn. "Hmmm," he mused as he closed the book and turned his light off, "it would be handy if Moses had written something like this!"

Biblical background
Read Hebrews 11 v 1 – 12 v 2

Hebrews 11 gives us a long list of great leaders. "Faith" is the repeated characteristic of these people.

? What did they have faith in (11 v 10-16, 39-40)?

? How did this faith impact how they acted?

? Who do these "great cloud of witnesses" ultimately point to (12 v 1-2)?

Read all about it

We began with the foundational truth that this is God's world and God rules. Genesis adds an important dimension to that rule: *God rules through his word.* Genesis 1 repeatedly refers to God speaking. The creation of man and woman are the fruit of a conversation. (*"Let us..."*, verse 26).

Adam

God also rules through others. God appoints the man and woman as his image-bearers to rule in his place, giving them a mandate to rule. God, the Leader, through his word appoints leaders. These are very important staging points in the whole process of under-standing leadership.

Devolved leadership enters into the picture very early on—before the fall. Leadership is not God's way of trying to handle the mess that we're in. Like marriage and community, it is a good thing that is there from the beginning.

Abraham

Throughout the early chapters of Genesis we find God dealing directly with the human race. Genesis 1 – 11 has been described as the prologue to the rest of the Bible. Chapter 12 comes directly after the incident at Babel, when the inhabitants of the world have been scattered. God sovereignly frustrates their intention to come together to make a name for themselves. God focuses down on one man—Abram—but only in order that he can bless all the nations (verses 1-3).

Abraham has a leadership role in the sense that he is to mediate God's blessings—he is the channel of God's blessing to the world. This role is clearly shown in Genesis 18 v 17-33, when God is about to act in judgment against Sodom and Gomorrah. God knows the appalling sin of Sodom and Gomorrah; he knows that they are ripe for judgment.

But Abraham is significant in what God does, and how he does it. In this remarkable conversation God lets Abraham see that he is neither vengeful nor irrational in his wrath. When he finally does judge Sodom and Gomorrah, he does so because he is a God of righteousness and justice.

Abraham is brought to the point where he sees God acting, so that when he speaks to his descendants about it, he can say that this is an act of God's righteous justice. Abraham's role is to teach his children God's character, and through this to bless the nations (see Exodus 19 v 5–6; Deuteronomy 4 v 5–8). That is also the role of leaders to teach God's people God's character.

Joseph

One of the key themes of Genesis is to trace the beginning of what we later learn is the family line of the Messiah from Adam to Abraham to David to Jesus (see Matthew 1; Luke 3). That line does not go *through* Joseph, but he has a very important responsibility and so has a substantial part of Genesis dedicated to him. He is the protector of the righteous line.

The early part of the story makes much of the leadership role of Joseph, beginning with his dream in chapter 37 in which he "sees" his family bowing down before him. That provokes the question of verse 8:

"Do you intend to reign over us? Will you actually rule us?"

In Egypt, although only a slave, Joseph is promoted to a top position of responsibility. When Joseph lands in prison, he is soon given responsibility for the rest of the prisoners (see 39 v 22-23). It is not too long before Joseph reaches the highest position in the land, second only to Pharaoh himself (see 41 v 38-45).

However, the purpose of this extended focus on Joseph is not to teach us about leadership or how to succeed. It performs the same function as the rest of the second half of Genesis, which is to demonstrate God's commitment to his promise to Abraham. The nations (eg: Egypt) are blessed through God's covenant faithfulness. Joseph is there to protect the people of promise and to guard the covenant promise.

Moses

The next significant person to be appointed to a position of leadership is Moses. Once again, the covenant is integral to the position, as Exodus 3 v 6-9 shows. God "remembers" his promise to Abraham—Moses is commissioned so that through him God can fulfil his purposes. Moses is raised up to rescue the covenant people, and like Joseph before him, to guard God's promise to Abraham.

Moses leads the people of promise through the Red Sea, via Mount Sinai, around the desert and right to the edge of the land of promise. It is clearly a significant leadership role, which is probably unsurpassed in the whole of the Old Testament. Central to the leadership of Moses is the word spoken by God at Sinai, where Israel is given God's law. Moses has responsibility for delivering that word to the people, and mediating God's rule and presence.

It seems that Moses is regarded as unique in his role (Deuteronomy 34 v 10). In Moses we have an example of leadership, but leadership in a covenant context. He's not our point of reference if we want to know how to lead. We could look to him for leadership guidance in very much the same way we could look to Winston Churchill or Nelson Mandela. But that's not the intent of the Bible here; Moses serves an altogether higher purpose. Moses' leadership is like the law itself, which, according to Matthew 5 v 17-20, is not our reference point when it comes to living a life that pleases God. Its function is to point to Jesus. So it is with Moses. He is a redemptive figure—a "type" of Jesus who rescues his people from captivity.

Prophet, priest, king and judge

Deuteronomy 16 v 18 – 18 v 22 is a crucial passage in terms of leadership, and highlights four categories of leaders: judge, priest, king and prophet.

These are not rescuers, but they do exercise leadership among the people of God. The key aspects of their leadership are found in 16 v 18; 17

v 11; 17 v 18-19 and 18 v 18, where each type of leadership role is framed as being based upon the word of God. God is still ruling his people, and ruling them through his word, as exercised by the "sub-leaders".

The king, for example, is presented as a model Israelite. He is to reject weapons, women and wealth, and pursue godliness as he sets the law before him and follows it in obedience. His primary role is to exemplify subservience to God's covenant. We could just say that this is a great example of leadership... *but that completely misses the point!* The law is not just our reference point for right and wrong; it is there to inform our understanding of who God is, and what it means to be in relationship with Him. Ultimately it reveals to us Jesus and his work. So the appointment of these leaders is again evidence of God's intention to lead his people through his word.

Nehemiah

The primary reason for highlighting Nehemiah in this list is because he is often used as an example of godly leadership. Yet we must remember his particular place within the biblical story. His role was in rebuilding the city of Jerusalem for the returnees, and reconstituting the people as God's people under God's word.

We can learn some important leadership principles from Nehemiah because there is something universal about them: he plans, he prays, he mobilizes the people and stands up to opposition well. However, as illuminating as they are, these leadership principles *cannot be what the book is fundamentally about.* We have to be sensitive to its historical setting, and mindful of the promises spoken to the people about their return.

In the final analysis, Nehemiah is a book of failure (13 v 6-31). For all his skill, leadership, passion and protestations, Nehemiah is incapable of producing godliness and obedience to the law. For all of the promise of Nehemiah, the hearts of the people remained unchanged.

As we will explore in the next chapter, Nehemiah points to the need for another leader—one who will be more successful in building the city of God and forming the people of God.

The central point of this chapter is that *God's rule is mediated.* God rules through his servants. The role of leaders is important in that they:

- **teach God's people** about the character of the God to whom they belong.
- **protect the people of promise** and guard the covenant promise.
- **deliver God's word to God's people** and mediate God's rule.
- **exemplify subservience** to God's covenant.
- **reconstitute the people** under God's word.
- **point to the need for another leader.**

To say that God's rule is mediated is not the same as saying that God has abdicated. God still rules, and he rules by his word. Characteristically, he appoints, and approves of, leaders who will teach his word and apply it meaningfully and specifically to the hearts and minds of his people. It is in this way that God guards the gospel—bringing both the promises to fulfilment, and the people to maturity and blessing.

Questions for reflection

? If you are in a position of leadership, how well do you think you mediate God's rule and point to King Jesus?

? Leaders must both know and submit to God's word if they are to be true to their calling to defend, promote and model the truth. If you are a leader, is reading the Scriptures part of your daily routine? What about those who lead you?

? Are you prepared to defend the gospel against those who twist it?

3 LEARNING FROM THE LEADER

Jesus is the ultimate Ruler.

Consider this

There was a collective sense of unease as the church prepared to discuss the appointment of two new elders. Everyone was persuaded that this was an important and necessary step, but what if they got it wrong? Two people in particular had been fairly vocal about their questions, and as the others listened, it had to be admitted that they had a point. Was there a job description for the elders' role? If there was, no one had taken the time or trouble to explain it. But surely it was important to know. Not only for the church as a whole, but also for the two "candidates"!

Biblical background
John 10 v 1-18, Psalm 23, Ezekiel 34

[?] In what two ways does Jesus describe his role as the leader in John 10 v 7-10 and 11-14?

[?] How does this relate to Psalm 23 and Ezekiel 34 v 23-24? What is Jesus saying?

[?] What characterizes false shepherds in Ezekiel 34 v 1-4?

[?] What does God promise to do in Ezekiel 34 v 11-16?

[?] How do John 10 v 11 and 15 help us understand how God will achieve what He promises in Psalm 23 and Ezekiel 34?

Read all about it

As you start to read the Old Testament, particularly through the lens of leadership, something very significant begins to stand out—all the "leaders" are utter failures!

Noah. Abraham. Moses. David. Nehemiah.

Drunkard. Coward. Murderer. Adulterer. Failure.

The list is both long and startling. They are all significant failures who fail significantly. In various ways and through various means they prove themselves to be unfit for the task given to them.

But as the Romans used to say, *nil desperandum* (never despair)! Admittedly, this would seem to be disappointing and profoundly depressing. But it turns out to be quite the opposite when we discover that this is how God intended it to be from the beginning.

These leaders are not simply an end in themselves. All the leaders in the Old Testament—the "good" ones in particular—point to, inform and prepare for the one true leader of God's people. Jesus incorporates all of the aspects of Old Testament leadership in his own person and he is the one to whom they were all pointing.

He lives as a model man and a model Israelite. He is filled with the Spirit without measure, he obeys the law, reveals God, rescues his people and sets the captives free. Jesus is the final Adam. He is the true Abraham, as the progenitor of a new nation. He is the true David, who rules as God's king. He is the true Judge, the true Priest, the true Prophet. Everything that the Old Testament says about leadership finds its glorious fulfilment in Jesus. In Him, God's rule is both mediated and direct. He is King Jesus, the Lord of heaven and earth and, as Revelation so clearly shows, *He rules!*

The picture of Jesus in Revelation 1 – 3 is of a mighty King who walks among his people, and exercises his rule over them. He has not abdicated, and he does not delegate his authority. His knowledge of his churches is intimate. Jesus rules through his word and by his Spirit.

It is worth pausing at this point to think about a besetting sin of many in church leadership. Young leaders in particular, show a reluctance or refusal to trust in the ability of Jesus to rule that is shown in how they view their leadership. Through inexperience or pride, leaders can overstretch themselves thinking that they themselves are to be a "savior" of God's people. They believe that it is up to them to make people godly, to sort out their problems, to rescue them from disaster. They get caught in a cycle of crippling workloads, a stressful sense of responsibility for others, and guilt and despair when they fail. Time and time again I have seen people who have become overwhelmed by the false task they have set themselves.

Instead, leaders need a quiet confidence in Jesus to rule through his word, by his Spirit. We need to teach and model the word of God. We need to get alongside people lovingly to encourage them and, where necessary, rebuke them. But all this is done in the confidence that it is Jesus who rules his church. He is the one to whom we are to look and he calls us to follow Him, and submit to his leadership, even in the way that we lead. He is the Servant King, and we are called to live as servant leaders—not lording it over the flock, but always behaving as under-shepherds.

The shepherd and the sheep

This introduces us to an important biblical image for leadership, that of *shepherd*. The biblical function of shepherds is to care and provide for, protect and lead their sheep. Good shepherds protect their sheep until death. In John 10, Jesus speaks at length of his identity as the Good Shepherd.

In using this image, Jesus is drawing on a rich biblical tradition (cf. Psalm 23, Ezekiel 34), and making a bold claim. As Ezekiel 34 shows, Israel had a history of "bad" shepherds, who were motivated by self-interest. They used their position to serve their own needs. They were not only apathetic about the flock they were appointed to serve, they were also indifferent to the One who owned the flock. They behaved like hired hands (John 10 v 12-13,) who viewed the sheep as nothing more than a disposable commodity.

In stark and noble contrast, Jesus is the Good Shepherd, who has intimate knowledge of his sheep, and is willing to lay down his life for them (v 11). He gathers up the lost and leads those who have no shepherd (Matthew 9 v 36). All those who belong to Christ are his sheep (John 21 v 16). He is the Shepherd for whom the sheep have been waiting; he is the one who fulfills God's promise to give Israel a true Shepherd (Ezekiel 34 v 11-31). He takes an active interest in them. Although he is "merely" the shepherd, he acts as if he owns the flock! Some shepherds may be willing to risk their lives for the sheep. But this good shepherd actually gives his life for the sheep.

There are two important things to take from this.

1. **God has graciously given his Son to shepherd his sheep.** This is an amazing provision, inspiring our heartfelt thanks! He is competent, caring and committed. There is no better flock to belong to than the one under the watchful eye of the Good Shepherd. Having laid down his life for his sheep, he takes it up again (John 10 v 17,18) and as the risen Lord, he remains the Shepherd of God's flock.

2. **Leadership among the people of God, in any context, should be modeled on that of Jesus.** Our leadership should look like His. He continues to actively lead, so our leadership ought not to be at odds with His—in either style or intent.

If the sheep are to be protected and guided so they flourish and prosper, they need a consistency of approach. Christ is the chief Shepherd, but leaders are to shepherd the flock too, providing an example for them (1 Peter 5 v 2-4). Biblically, pastoral imagery is very important in any consideration of leadership. One writer on the subject says that "shepherd leadership is comprehensive in its scope". He goes on to explain the shepherd role as "protector, provider and guide", and that "the task of shepherds is determined daily by the changing needs of the flock under their care".[1] The true shepherd cares for his flock and protects them; so, as under-shepherds, we need to learn from the supreme Shepherd as we care for our people.

---

1   Laniak, Timothy, S., Shepherds After Mine Own Heart, Apollos: Illinios, 2006, 247

This picture is vital when we encounter a word like "headship", which can sound threatening and, in a western culture particularly, authoritarian. But as the Good Shepherd, Jesus exercises headship over the flock of God. The issue is not headship *per se*, but how that headship is exercised.

What is headship?

In simple terms, headship is all about **creating an environment in which those in our care are able to flourish and thrive**, becoming all that God intends them to be as they use their gifts for his glory and the good of others. In fact, those in positions of responsibility are a vital means of that happening.

When Paul was writing to Titus, instructing him in how to combat false teaching among the churches in Crete, his first task was to appoint elders. Leaders were vital to those churches being gospel-centered churches. But it was not only the *fact* of leadership but the *type* of leader that was important. Which is why Paul highlights the key characteristics of leaders, looking at how they exercise headship in their home, their relationship with their wives, the behavior of their children and their reputation among their neighbors.

It is worth saying at this point that when writing to Timothy and Titus concerning the appointment of elders, Paul assumes they will be male. This does not preclude women from positions of responsibility and influence. The New Testament has many references to women "in ministry", eg: Phoebe, Euodia, Syntyche and Priscilla.

Furthermore, it is important to recognize that **all Christian women are gospel ministers**. But headship in the home and in the local church is *always male*. This is not the place to go into the arguments for and against this position, but simply to say that, if the way headship is exercised reflects the headship of Jesus, then many of the objections to leadership in general and male leadership in particular become redundant.

There are many Bible characters who are attractive and offer insight into our leadership roles and responsibilities. There may be many ideas, principles and techniques which we can usefully learn from modern leadership literature and gurus. But the bedrock model for our leadership must always be and remain the Lord Jesus.

Questions for reflection

❓ What, in your opinion, are the strengths and weaknesses of how your church is led at the moment?

❓ Think of some leaders in your cultural setting — these might be economic, civic, national, or church leaders, or supervisors at work. Do they display any characteristics of Jesus' leadership? If you are ever frustrated with them, is it because they fall short of Jesus' model?

❓ If you are in a position of leadership (in the family, in the church community, in the workplace), do you exercise your authority in a Christ-like manner?

❓ Think about the "sheep" you have responsibility for. You will never know them as Jesus knows them, but are you making every effort to understand them, and to know about their circumstances—their troubles and joys?

❓ Do you know what dangers your "sheep" are facing? What particular temptations are they vulnerable to? How can you help protect them?

❓ Do you truly love your "sheep"?
Would you be prepared to die for them?

PART TWO

DISTINCTIVES

Gospel-centered leadership

4 CHARACTER

Principle

The chief qualification for Christian leadership is a godly character.

Consider this

Sam sat listening to his friend, the impressive mega-church preacher, with a growing sense of inadequacy.

His friend was funny, quick witted, eloquent, charming ... able to preach a brilliant Bible talk to a packed room in a way that would surely win over the most hardened atheist!

Sam sighed.

He couldn't help wondering why he'd been given a position of leadership in his church. He didn't have any of the charisma and beaming confidence of his friend, though he loved Jesus and loved seeing the Holy Spirit change people through the word. Was that simple, though sincere, desire enough to qualify him for his role?

Biblical background
1 Timothy 3 v 1-7; Titus 1 v 6-9

☐ Make a list of what an elder must be.

☐ Make a list of what an elder must not be.

☐ Do you find anything surprising about these two lists?

☐ How do these lists match up with how you assess leaders in your church?

Read all about it

Before we see how character is the key component of leadership, it will be helpful to clear the ground by considering briefly the terms used in the Bible to describe leadership.

PROPHET/PRIEST/KING/JUDGE: As we have seen, these are all functions and offices that point primarily to Jesus and are fulfilled in him. Nowhere in the New Testament are leaders of churches referred to, or described by, any of these titles. And for a good, gospel reason.

Under the new covenant, all of God's people are both prophets and priests. We are prophets because we are "in Christ", the true Prophet. As his people we speak the word of God into each others lives with Holy-Spirit given authority and conviction.

We are priests because we are "in Christ", the true Priest. As his people we bring one another before the Father in prayer, and by the Holy Spirit we are a means of grace to others as we mediate God's love in and through our relationships.

Paul also, somewhat strikingly, asserts that Christians are appointed as judges (1 Corinthians 6 v 2). It is our role to call the world to account for it's failure and refusal to submit to God's command to everyone, everywhere to repent (Acts 17 v 30).

APOSTLES: This term is used principally to describe those appointed by Jesus and who were witnesses of the resurrection. This group, which included Paul as 'one untimely born', had a foundational and unique role.

It was also applied to others outside this group, but these need to be differentiated from the foundational apostles in terms of significance and weight.

Are there apostles today? In the secondary sense, it is difficult to see why that would not be the case. But the problem we have is that there is very little in the Bible that tells us what an apostle "with a small a" looks like or even what one does! Because of this, a great deal of material about contemporary apostles imports concepts and ideas from outside the Bible. Which means that it may or may not be right, but there is no sure way of knowing.

Even the oft cited passage in Ephesians 4 and the so-called "five-fold APEST ministries" seems to be primarily illustrative for Paul of his primary concern that it is the body as a whole that is to grow into maturity and be effective for Christ in the world.

Wisdom teaches that we should take great care in building an elaborate structure on an insubstantial foundation.

EVANGELISTS: Again, one or two evangelists are referenced in the NT, but almost nothing is said of them by way of their role or function. They clearly have something to do with the gospel or good news, because that is the root meaning of the title. But does that mean that they are the primary proclaimers of the evangel? Or that they are the "gospel midwives" in that they just happen to be around more than most when new believers are born again? What we do know is that they are to equip the saints for works of service because that is what Ephesians 4 v 11-12 tells us. Beyond that we just don't know anything for certain.

DEACON: This is role within the local church as Paul teaches about it in 1 Timothy 3 v 8-13. He addresses deacons along with bishops in his opening address to the believers in Philippi (Philippians 1 v 1). It seems they have a an important and supportive role as those who assist the elders in their responsibilities and in taking a lead in the practical issues of care.

PASTOR (TEACHER)/ELDER/BISHOP: As John Stott has pointed out so definitively, these are three roles of the same "office". A pastor is an elder who is also a bishop. A bishop is a pastor who is an elder. An elder is a bishop who is a pastor. You get the drift I'm sure!

• **Pastor** means shepherd and refers to the manner of leadership.

- **Elder** highlights maturity and so status and highlights the gravity of leadership.
- **Bishop** means one who has oversight and refers to the scope of leadership.

As we shall see in a later chapter, the term pastor is the dominant motif in the New Testament for leadership, and so should exercise a defining influence on our view of, practice of, and response to leadership.

Qualifications

The biblical qualifications for leadership are really quite simple. A leader must have **a godly character** and **an aptitude to teach**. Full stop. Leaders influence the people of God as they teach God's word and as they model obedience to God's word in their lives.

Many leaders are uncomfortable with 1 Corinthians 11 v 1: *"Imitate me as I imitate Christ"*.

We're happy for Paul to say it (he was, after all, an apostle), but we feel very awkward saying it about ourselves… we are far too modest ever to hint at such a thing! But I want to suggest that our awkwardness reflects not so much our modesty as our reluctance to take seriously the requirements of leaders to be examples. Paul says in Philippians 3 v 12-17:

> Not that I have already obtained all this, or have already been made perfect, but I press on to take hold of that for which Christ Jesus took hold of me … Only let us live up to what we have already attained. Join with others in following my example, brothers, and take note of those who live according to the pattern we gave you.

Humility does not stop Paul asserting that his way of life and his teaching are in complete harmony. Paul claims that it is right for the Corinthians to look at him and imitate him. He says the same again in 2 Thessalonians 3 v 6-10:

> Now we command you, brothers, in the name of our Lord Jesus Christ

that you keep away from any brother who is walking in idleness and not in accord with the tradition that you received from us. For you yourselves know how you ought to imitate us, because we were not idle when we were with you, nor did we eat anyone's bread without paying for it, but with toil and labor we worked night and day, that we might not be a burden to any of you. It was not because we do not have that right, but to give you in ourselves an example to imitate.

Notice the use of the pronouns *we*, not *I*. Paul was not pointing to himself because he was one of an elite; he was drawing attention to all the apostles, and how they corporately modeled gospel living to those around them.

In Paul's mind, providing lived examples of the gospel is a key strategy for discipleship. In a sermon on 1 Thessalonians 2, Don Carson once asked this haunting question:

"When the last time was that we went up to someone and said: 'You want to know what a life lived for the gospel looks like? Well, watch me!'"

He then went on to say that if we don't do this, we are neglecting our responsibilities. The bottom line is this: as leaders we are called to be examples. Being an example is the primary way we lead. We are called to be intentional in how we live so that we can commend our attitude and lifestyle to others.

To highlight these points, consider Paul's words to his young apprentices, Timothy and Titus:

Do not let anyone look down on you because you are young, but set an example for the believers in speech, in life, in love, in faith and in purity. Be diligent in these matters; give yourself wholly to them, so that everyone may see your progress. Watch your life and doctrine closely. Persevere in them, because if you do, you will save both yourself and your hearers. (1 Timothy 4 v 12, 15-16)

There were two principal matters of which Timothy had to be

mindful: the word of God and a life transformed by the word of God. It was his responsibility to give due weight to both the word of God as he taught it and the word of God as he lived it. In fact, it was only through persevering in *both* life *and* doctrine that he would save himself and those for whom he was responsible.

It is clear from verse 11 that Timothy's example is seen in every part of his life: speech, conduct, love, faith and purity.[2] Commentators suggest that the first two (speech and conduct) relate to Timothy's public ministry, and the final three (love, faith and purity) to the details of his own life. Or, the first two give the sphere and the final three the qualities in which he is to be a model.

But I am not at all persuaded that you can drive a knife between the public and the private. Paul's whole point is that **there is no possible separation**: integrity means that there is no difference between who we are in private and who we are in public. That is why in 1 Timothy 3, the qualities of an elder are forged in the workshop of the home and family life: as a man leads his family, so he leads the church.

A man's character is seen in all of his life. Timothy's example is to be comprehensive. In every aspect of life you are to be an example. This means that as leaders, you are to demonstrate what you teach by how you live. In this way, the gospel you commend to others is the gospel you commend to yourself; the gospel that you want to change other people's hearts is the gospel that has changed your heart. It is more likely to have that impact on others when it has first had that impact on you and when others can see its fruit in your life.

But it is also vital we note that Timothy's godliness is to be progressive. John Stott says:

The example which Christian leaders set then, whether in their
life or their ministry, should be dynamic and progressive. People
should be able to observe not only what they *are*, but *what they are
becoming*, supplying evidence that they are growing into maturity in

---

2 Although there may be a contextual element to this list—these are the virtues conspicuously absent
   from the lives of the false teachers in Ephesus—they nonetheless retain a universal application.

Christ. Some leaders imagine that they have to appear perfect, with no visible flaws or blemishes. There are two reasons why this is a mistake. First, it is hypocritical. Second, the pretense discourages people who then suppose that their leaders are altogether exceptional or even inhuman.[3]

Timothy is a leader in the church; in fact he is there in the place of the Apostle Paul. But that does not mean that he asserts his authority or throws his weight around. What he does is get godly! In discussing the Greek word translated example in 1 Timothy 4 v 12, William Mounce makes this intriguing comment: *"the word picture it paints is not so much that Timothy is an example that others can emulate but that he is a mold that should be pressed into the lives of others so that they can attain the same shape."* [4]

Calvin makes these helpful observations: [5]

For our part, what else have we to do, but walk in such a way that the doctrine we believe is proved true to the world by how we live? Paul also says that those who are the leaders must set an example in spirit [life], that they must have a special liveliness above others … This liveliness and quickness the apostle speaks is in order that they might demonstrate to others the right way to live. We need a better taste of God's promises than we had before, more careful and earnest prayer, better resistance to temptation and worldly attitudes, that we might live holy lives. His behavior must be proof of the very doctrine he preaches. He must edify others in all that he does.

A range of NT verses demonstrate the same emphasis:

In everything set them an example by doing what is good. In your teaching show integrity, seriousness and soundness of speech

3 J. R. W. Stott, *Guard the Truth: the message of 1 Timothy and Titus* (IVP, 1996), p.123
4 W. D. Mounce, *Pastoral Epistles* (Vol. 46, Word Biblical Commentary; Thomas Nelson, 2000),
5 Drawn from John Calvin's Sermons on Timothy and Titus (originally published 1579). Available online at http://www.puritansermons.com

> that cannot be condemned, so that those who oppose you may be ashamed because they have nothing bad to say about us. **Titus 2 v 6-8**
>
> To the elders among you, I appeal as a fellow elder … Be shepherds of God's flock that is under your care, serving as overseers—not because you must, but because you are willing, as God wants you to be; not greedy for money, but eager to serve; not lording it over those entrusted to you, but being examples to the flock. **1 Peter 5 v 1-3**

Leadership is always about encouraging people to do what I do, and not simply to hear and do what I say. This is why godly character is essential: it demonstrates where the real authority lies. The task of a leader is to teach the word of God. That word is to be applied in the first instance to my own life, and I am to live under it and be shaped by it. That way, people will see that it is Christ, not me, who rules his church!

Questions for reflection

- Do you feel uncomfortable with 1 Corinthians 11:1: *Imitate me as I imitate Christ?"* Why?
- How can you be an example to others in areas that you don't think you are gifted in?
- If your church or small group grew to be disciples just like you, what would it look like? What would it excel at? What would it be poor at? How does this help you shape your attitude towards your own Christian growth and discipleship?
- In what ways is your Christian life visible to the sheep in your care? How could you make it more so?
- How can you urge people to imitate you without appearing egocentric?

5 APTITUDE

Principle

You can't put in what God left out.

Consider this

The church elders were weighing up Glen's leadership potential.

"He clearly loves the Lord," said John.

"Yes, and he looks after his wife and family well and shows a deep care for his brothers and sisters," added David.

Mark thought for a moment before he chipped in. "Look, I know he's keen to initiate activities and always very responsive in group Bible studies—but do you think he *really* has an aptitude for teaching God's word?"

It was silent round the table for a while before John asked the obvious question: "What does that kind of aptitude look like in practice?

Biblical background
1 Timothy 3:2; Titus 1:9-16

❓ What one skill does Paul say an elder must have (1 Tim 3:2)?

❓ To do this Paul says that an elder must "hold firmly to the trustworthy message as it has been taught". What will this enable him to do (Titus 1:9)?

❓ Why is this so important (1:10-16)?

❓ What is the desired result of an elder exercising this skill (1:13)?

Read all about it

Are leaders born or made?

One of the things I have been arguing strongly in this book is that our view of Christian leadership is often flawed and compromised by our cultural conditioning of what we think leadership ought to look like.

The criteria laid out in the Scriptures for local-church leadership are really very simple.

A **godly lifestyle** and an **ability to teach**.

But are these qualities hard-wired into us like a basic ability to kick a football, roll your tongue or hold a tune; or can they be developed from unpromising material?

The answer is, of course, *both*.

There are some basic aptitudes that seem to be inherent to the way we are put together as individuals. They are just the way God, in his wisdom and sovereign purposes, has made us for his glory. There are some things that, because of temperament, gifting, disposition— call it what you will—we will *never* have an instinct for. I think it is literally true of some things that **you can't put in what God left out.**

But these qualities can be dormant and under-developed in people. And there are pastoral-leadership qualities that have been perverted by our sinfulness into traits that are ugly, but that can be redeemed by the careful application of the gospel, and the work of the Holy Spirit in our hearts.

These are the thoughts that run through my mind as I fellowship with people at church or in small groups, and observe them in action. I am always looking for potential leaders. When I see these qualities on show, I ask myself: How can I invest in this person? How can I test this ability? How can I help it grow?

For the rest of this chapter I want to think about six aptitudes that I think are important in leadership. I am not saying that someone needs to have all of these to be a leader, but they are the key things that I look out for, and try to encourage and train people to develop.

Sometimes we see these gifts perverted.

Sometimes they are conspicuous by their complete absence. But learning to recognize them will help enormously.

And if you are reading this book, not as a church leader to think about training other church leaders, but as someone wondering whether leadership is something God is calling you to, then use this list to make a sober assessment of your abilities, and to spur you on to grow.

1. An aptitude to teach

To repeat. Our culture makes the assumption:

Good preacher = Christian leader.

But an ability to teach isn't oratory: the ability to make a rhetorical flourish, or to hold a crowd. There are plenty of people who can do all those things, who actually fail to teach effectively. **It's the more fundamental ability to bring the truths of God's word to bear with relevance into people's lives**. And the truth is that this happens more often in a conversation than in a pulpit.

When you break this ability down into its component parts, yes there are elements of an ability with words, a grasp of doctrine, and an understanding of how people work and think. But there are also elements of courage, and a conviction and confidence that the word of God in the gospel is the one thing that will truly help others.

Calvin said: *"The purpose of Scripture is to do us good."*
That's the most insightful comment I have ever heard in terms of shaping my own ministry. It overtly shapes everything I do. What masquerades as good teaching is sometimes a well-crafted sermon, or Sunday-school lesson, a well-led Bible study, a presentation of the Bible that is polished and balanced.

But as a hearer, you have to work hard to get the goodness out of it. Those with an ability to teach will bring the Scripture to bear on someone's life in a way that does them good. They are able to make it plain, make it real. To get to people's hearts under the radar of their defences. Let me give an example.

I'd been teaching a pastoral-care course to the leaders of a church, and had been talking about applying the gospel to your heart. On the drive back from the church to where I was staying, one young guy asked me: "Steve, are there any areas that you struggle with in terms of fears?"

It was a bold question, given that I was the mature experienced pastor, and he was in his early 20s. I shared with him an irrational fear I have of being on my own in a house at night. I've always thought it weird, because I am not generally a fearful person.

I was thrilled when he started to gospel me. Gently, but with a determination that showed he had a confidence in God's word, he tried to bring the truth of the gospel to bear on my heart. He demonstrated a real aptitude to teach. Even though he was younger, he had the courage to do it in a respectful way, just as Paul urged Timothy to do (see 1 Tim 4 v 12; 5 v 1).

2. An aptitude for taking responsibility

The Good Shepherd shows the pattern for us, and he is proactive on caring for and protecting the sheep.

Responsibility is often shown in small ways. You can recognize it in people who show that they want to take part in what is going on at a meeting—they are not there to be passengers.

So at a prayer meeting, they will fill a silence by taking the initiative and praying out loud. At a church service, before and after, they will look for what needs to be done, and get on with it. They will not just sit by and do nothing just because they don't have an assigned role for the day.

And this can be at the simplest level—seeing if the bin needs emptying, spotting someone who looks new and talking with them, getting up and fetching a book for someone who does not have one.

But this is not just an individual sense of responsibility. They will also have an aptitude and an instinct for mobilizing others in the work. Rather than just put all the chairs out themselves, they will want to draw others into the work. They will recognize that this simple act of service is also *a moment to disciple others.*

Virtues and vices

Virtues are often their own vices. And at its worst, this good instinct to take responsibility can easily become control freakery. I can think that only I can do it well enough. I can be frustrated at the inability of others to join in, or to do it well enough. It can spring from, not a desire to serve Jesus out of thankfulness for his service to me, but from a self-loving, self-worshiping legalism. It can simply show that I do not trust in God's sovereignty.

We need to remember that perfectionism is a sin. It doesn't live with the reality of a fallen world. And what should be a demonstration of my love for God in the way I love and serve others ends up being *"all about me"*.

Where the instinct to take responsibility is lacking we see a whole range of attitudes. Of course, there will always be those who cruise, and let others take the strain, when they ought to be more involved.

But there are also those who are vocal in their criticism, and spend their time blaming others for the failings of the church. Or those who contribute interesting and creative ideas, but think that this alone is their contribution, because they are not willing to actually do them. It may have many faces, but it comes down to the same thing. If someone is not willing to take responsibility then they are simply not suitable to develop in leadership—whatever their other gifts may be.

3. An aptitude for influencing people

To influence someone is to shape them. It's to re-orientate them so that their values change, and their ambitions are shaped by God's word. It is the motivation for teaching others. Not so that they would have more information about the Bible, but that God's word would result in their transformation. So that they become centered on the gospel and not on themselves.

You don't need institutional power to do that. Influence is often wielded through quiet conversations. Through a pithy soundbite over coffee. Through a willingness to share your own struggles, joys and insights in your discipleship. By demonstrating the priority of the gospel in the life choices you make.

In a Bible study, this instinct will be evident in someone who seeks to influence the way the conversation moves. By the way they answer questions and encourage others to speak.

It will be evident in the way we encourage each other to be bold in evangelism, and share our new visions, new horizons, new ideas.

To be a leader is to be an influencer for the sake of Christ, and to be delighted when you see people follow Him, even if they do not share your particular views on everything.

Virtues and vices

But, as we have seen, virtues are often their own vices. Being an influencer can feed our own ego as we work to clone ourselves in others, rather than see Christ grow uniquely in them. It can be power wielded to assert your control over others. Or, like Professor Slughorn at Hogwarts in *Harry Potter*, to bask in the reflected glory of others. We need to remember that those in our care are not *our disciples*, they are *Christ's disciples*.

Where this instinct is absent we see an indifference towards others that can masquerade as professionalism, or just being cool. At heart, when people show no ambition for other people's godliness, they are simply demonstrating that they love themselves, not others.

4. An aptitude for people.

Ministry and leadership is a people business. And people are not commodities or resources to be bought and sold. Jesus is the Good Shepherd, and we model all our leadership on Him. He loves the sheep, he knows the sheep by name, he calls the sheep out by name and they follow Him. A true pastor is going to imitate those characteristics. He will love people and get to know people.

In John 10, Jesus compares Himself with the bad shepherds, who only have a concern for themselves, and abandon the sheep when there is danger. So a key question to ask of potential leaders is a simple one: *Do they genuinely love people?*

And is that demonstrated by a concern to know and understand them, and a loyalty to them that goes beyond enjoyment of their company in good times.

That doesn't mean you need to be a great socialite, or the life and soul of the party.

At its worst, a connection with people can reveal that you are needy, and that you need people to respond to you, or affirm you in order to feel good about yourself. Godly maturity means that you will be content with your own company and happy in a crowd.

You will observe the absence of this quality when you think of people as an annoyance and an intrusion. When people are a hindrance to achieving what you want to achieve.

5 An aptitude for hard work:
In 1 Thessalonians 2 Paul commends himself by saying :

> For you remember, brothers, our labor and toil: we worked night
> and day, that we might not be a burden to any of you, while we
> proclaimed to you the gospel of God.

Paul carried animal skins around and stitched away making tents during the day, and then did gospel work at night. The Lord Jesus endured a punishing schedule. Just read through Mark 1 v 21-35 to track a typical day. Christian leadership involves hard work.

I tell those in leadership in the church I am part of that I want them to work *at least as hard* as members of the congregation. That means *at least* a 40-hour week. We have teachers, shop workers, doctors, drivers and businessmen who come to an early-morning prayer meeting, and who lead home Bible studies and serve at church on Sundays, while managing the daily grind of family and working life. We should not expect in full-time ministry to work any less hard.

For Christian leadership you have to be a bit of a self starter. Because much of the daily grind of preparation and pastoral work is invisible to most people, you can get away with doing very little. We need people who can get themselves out of bed without having to clock in and work a set time. It is the drive to work hard that demonstrates your credibility, integrity and commitment in Christian leadership.

But at its worst, hard work can be mere activism—a form of justification by works. We can make our business and tiredness into a virtue that fuels self-pity, and seeks the sympathy and recognition of others.

Laziness may not only show itself by an addiction to the Xbox, reading novels or hanging around with friends; it can also wear a deceptive mask. Sometimes people who appear busy can in fact be lazy—sometimes, people who go the gym a lot can be bone idle in the real work of building the body of Christ. Sometimes we in ministry can complain of fatigue after back-to-back pastoral meetings in Starbucks. We have confused hard gospel ministry with drinking lattes.

What we are hunting for are the young men who will turn up early to meetings and stay late. Who are prepared to offer lifts to people out of their area. We are looking for the women will give up time to others at their own cost. Who will stay up late or rise early to prepare their lesson for Sunday school on top of a demanding job. These are the ones who we will seek to invest in, to test and encourage.

6. An aptitude for self awareness

I think self awareness is an unspoken part of an ability to teach. Leaders need to have an ability to understand themselves and what their own issues are, because this is the skill which will enable them to empathize and understand the struggles of others, and so apply the gospel to them effectively. *Application always starts at home.* In leadership of any kind, unless we are in the habit of applying the Bible to ourselves, we will never be effective teachers to others.

At its worst, this quality makes for intense, self-absorbed people who are prone to self pity. At its best, it makes for confident mature Christians who have an unshakeable trust in their forgiveness in Christ, and are aware of their own blind spots and weaknesses.

True humility is a sober assessment of your gifts and vulnerabilities. Some of us are also good at *false humility*; somehow we think it is virtuous for us to claim that we are "just average". *"I do my best, but I nearly always make a hash of it."* This is simply not realistic.

The reverse is that you are always in the business of trying to push yourself forward. You see yourself as a commodity and you are always trying to sell yourself. Diffidence can be attractive. Pushiness can be downright ugly. True humility is different, but is essential for effective long-term leadership.

Am I made of the right stuff?

As I said at the start, these aptitudes are not an infallible guide, but I hope I have shown how they are connected components of the two vital qualifications of leadership—godliness and an ability to teach.

We don't want a cookie-cutter approach to leadership, which tries to produce clones. We want men and women who know their Lord, are confident in the gospel and who Jesus has called by name—that is, as the people with the personalities and the gifts that God Himself has given us.

The history of the church is full of people who would not have been considered "nice men", and yet in God's mercy they have been incredibly used in gospel ministry. Those of us with the responsibility of developing and shaping new leaders need to bear that in mind.

We need to remember that God is in control, and that *"we are his workmanship, created in Christ Jesus for good works, which God prepared beforehand, that we should walk in them"* (Ephesians 2 v 10).

Everything I have done in ministry, God has prepared in advance for me to do. The way I am wired is part of the way he develops me for these good works. Including my strengths and weaknesses in reflecting the perfect leader—the Good Shepherd.

And if you are reading this as someone who is wondering whether Christian leadership is for you, don't let your weakness in any of these areas make you feel you are disqualified. If you think this may be for you, then talk to your leaders. Ask them to help you grow and develop in the areas you need to. Ask them to test you and encourage you. And ask the Lord to help you grow in these areas, and so grow you into someone who is fit to bear the responsibility and privilege of being an under-shepherd in God's church.

 Questions for reflection

If you are a leader in your church...

🅑 Which of these six aptitudes do you think you have? Why?

🅑 Which ones do you think may be missing or perverted?

🅑 How could you be helped to develop these missing ones?

🅑 What can you do to help train and develop potential leaders in your church?

If you think God may be calling you to church leadership...

🅑 Which of these six aptitudes do you think you have? Why?

🅑 Which ones do you think may be missing or perverted?

🅑 Which leaders in your church could you seek help from the investigate your leadership potential?

🅑 Are you prepared to accept a possible decision that you are not leadership material? Why?

🅑 Are you ready for the hard work of training and developing these aptitudes?

6 WISDOM

Principle

The fear of the Lord is the beginning of wisdom.

Consider this

Tim smiled as he tucked his phone away and walked towards the shops. He was so thankful for his small-group leader. A situation had come up and Tim really hadn't been sure what to do about it, so he had phoned David with the question. In a few pithy words had given him a new perspective on the problem, and a way forward. The light-hearted, timely wisdom of his friend again pointed him in the right direction.

Mark was saddened following his conversation with Jeff, a young man in his small group. Jeff was determined to pursue a relationship with a girl who didn't seem to want any involvement in their church. Mark, after discussing it with the other elders, counseled Jeff to step back from the relationship. The conversation didn't go well—it was clear that Jeff thought he knew best.

Biblical background
Proverbs 1 v 1-7; 2 Corinthians 5 v 11

- ❓ Why did Solomon write the book of Proverbs (Proverbs 1 v 2-4)?
- ❓ What is the "beginning" or main component of wisdom/ knowledge/discipline (1 v 7)?
- ❓ What fruit does wisdom (fearing God) produce in Paul (2 Corinthians 5 v 11)?
- ❓ Why do you think fearing God enables Paul to do this?
- ❓ What lessons are there for you in this?

Read all about it

Wisdom is an important trait for a leader. The book of Proverbs paints some powerful pictures of wisdom:

- **Wise people use words to bless rather than curse;** their words are an effective indicator of a wise and an understanding heart.
- **Wise people recognize temptation and refuse to be seduced by sin;** their integrity reveals a wise and understanding heart.
- **Wise people listen to counsel and instruction;** their humility shows a wise and understanding heart.
- **Wise people are not quickly angry;** their self-control comes from a wise and understanding heart.

But from where does this wisdom come? Where can we find it, and how can we acquire it? What does wisdom look like in the everyday details of life? How do we spot it in others?

Proverbs 1 v 1-7 outlines the purpose of the proverbs of Solomon. They are in order to help people attain "wisdom and discipline" in "understanding words of insight, acquiring a disciplined and prudent life, doing what is right and just and fair." Solomon's proverbs are intended to "give prudence to the simple, knowledge and discretion to the young" and his plea is that the wise would "listen and add to their learning ... the discerning get guidance for understanding proverbs and parables, the sayings and riddles of the wise." Then the thesis statement for the whole book comes in verse 7:

"The fear of the LORD is the beginning of knowledge, but fools despise wisdom and discipline."

The intended benefit of Proverbs is to give wisdom, discipline, insight, knowledge and discernment. All of those attributes can be demonstrated in the nitty-gritty business of everyday life, and "wisdom" is the umbrella term to describe them all. It is the essential ingredient for living a good and fruitful life—wisdom is how we live well. This is particularly true for those of us who are leaders.

The word translated "beginning" means the "main component', or the chief element. The main component of wisdom is "the fear of the LORD". Fearing the LORD is the definition of wisdom. It is impossible to be wise without knowing, loving, honoring and worshiping God. Wise people fear God; people who fear God are wise.

Remember that "fear", in this context, is not cringing terror that forces you into a corner and leaves you a cowering wreck. "Fear" is awe, reverence, respect and regard. Fear is sensing the weightiness of someone or something. You fear that which is significant, and the greater your sense of the significance of someone or something, the greater your sense of fear. Wisdom is fearing God.

Everyone fears something or someone all of the time. As leaders who seek to be wise, we must fear the LORD. To summarize:

- Fearing the LORD is the main element of wisdom.
- Fearing anything else is the main element of foolishness.
- Fearing the LORD is the only way to lead well.
- Fearing anything or anyone else means that we will lead badly.

Alternative fears

What are leaders likely to fear instead of God? Many things, but this is perhaps the most significant.

We fear people!

Again, to "fear" people does not mean we are afraid of them in the way that we now use that term; we're not necessarily afraid that they might hit us or shout at us. Rather, fearing people means that they dominate our vision—they are disproportionately large in our thoughts and estimation. As a result, their opinion matters to us more than it should. Fearing people shapes our actions, and so we fail to live wisely and well.

This is the theological explanation for what is commonly known as "peer pressure". We reverence other people; we hold them in awe, and we crave their affirmation or admiration. Leaders who fear people will never be willing to challenge, rebuke or refute those who are straying or in error—and as unpleasant as those tasks may be, they are all biblical mandates. See if you recognize yourself in either of these two negative responses:

1. **We allow the expectations of other people to shape our behavior by conforming to their values.** For example, in a work situation the culture may be to work long hours, or to cut corners, or trim costs. The expectation is that you will "fit in", and because you "fear" your colleagues or boss, that is what you'll do. It may be slow and incremental, but it will happen over time. Whatever you fear will shape and define your life.

2. **We allow their expectations to shape our behavior by becoming despondent.** For example, no matter how much we try, we find we can't quite get into the "in crowd"; we can't quite manage to manoeuvre our way into the "inner circle". So when we fail to win their approval, or they fail to affirm or admire us, we become depressed and despondent. We fear them so much and crave their opinion so badly that we lose our sense of joy and perspective when we can't get what we think we need from them.

But what Proverbs asserts all the way through is that this is the way of folly.

A fool fears other people, and fearing others leads to foolish behavior: bad judgment calls, wrong turns and distorted ways of looking at life and reality.

Whatever we fear will shape and define our life. That is why fearing the Lord is the main element of wisdom. When we fear the Lord, everything else is in perspective, occupying its proper place in the scheme of things—they are neither too big nor too small.

At heart, Proverbs 1 v 7 is a call to worship. It is Solomon saying to Israel, and God saying to us: *Here is your God! Look at him in all of his glory, his holiness and his majestic splendor, and fear Him. Consider all that he has done for you. Listen to what he has said to you. Look at the deeds he has performed on your behalf. Take all of these on board, let*

them sink into your mind and heart, and stir your affections and "fear"
him because you shall then have nothing else to fear.

Wisdom in practice

As leaders, what are we tempted to fear other than the Lord God?
There are a myriad of possibilities, but consider these: reputation,
opinions of others, status, power and popularity.

We want to be esteemed as leaders. We want our people to respect
and listen to us. We want our fellow leaders to see how able we are
to teach God's word. We don't want people to think badly of us—to
think we're controlling, or manipulative, or weak. Perhaps we want
to maintain a certain persona or image. The very nature of leadership
means that leaders are inevitably in the spotlight—behavior, words,
and actions are seen and evaluated by many. There is clearly biblical
precedent for this—leaders are judged by a high standard and lead as
those who must give account to God for their work shepherding his
people. But when the scales get tipped and we begin to fear people
more than God, we are no longer leading with wisdom.

> *You're in the process of writing your first book. You want it to be*
> *edifying and well regarded by your peers, and haven't taken a weekend*
> *off for a few months because there's always more to do to get it right …*
> *much to the disappointment of your family and the detriment of your*
> *involvement in the people of God.*

Fear the approval of others and you live a stress-filled, lonely life
until publication.

Fear the LORD and you live wisely and well.

> *You and the other elders of your church need to make a difficult*
> *decision which could involve confrontation with people in the church,*
> *but is a gospel issue.*

Fear the opinions of church members and you dabble in heresy.

Fear the LORD and you live wisely and well.

*You're studying for your degree. It would mean a lot to you if you got
a top grade—but you know you're going to have to work very hard to
achieve it. For long periods throughout the term work takes up virtually
all your week. Relationships will have to take a back seat.*

Fear your status and the library is going to be your home from
home.

Fear the LORD and you will live well and wisely.

*You know that new laptop is ridiculously expensive, but it is quality,
and the name on it will get you a few admiring glances at the next
conference you attend.*

Fear your conference companions and your bank balance suffers.

Fear the LORD and live wisely and well.

A living example

Again we turn to Jesus—the true Shepherd and our model for
leading his people. Jesus was the wisest man to ever live. Why?
Because he feared the LORD! He loved him with all his heart, soul,
mind and strength. And because he feared the Lord, he had nothing
and no-one else to fear. his reputation meant nothing to Him. Fame
meant nothing to Him. Money meant nothing to Him. His life
meant nothing to Him. He "feared the Lord" in the sense that he
held his Father in awe and reverence. It was his Father's opinion
that mattered to him above that of anyone else. God was big and so
people were just the right size!

The result was that he lived wisely and well. He lived a rounded
life, in which he reached out to others, engaged with friends, chal-
lenged the corrupt authorities, lived vulnerably and simply and
allowed others to use and abuse Him. He lived an attractive and
compelling life because he feared the Lord. But notice this: he also
died a horrible death … and so have many of his followers.

Here's the problem: "Fearing the Lord" and living wisely and well in a manner consistent with that fear puts you out on a limb with the rest of society. At best, you're something of a misfit and an oddball. At worst, you're an irritant and annoyance.

The only thing that will sustain you when that annoyance spills over into active persecution of some kind is fearing the Lord. Fear him and the world is unable to either intimidate or seduce you. Fear him, the God who in history, his Word and supremely in Christ, has shown himself to be worthy of our love, reverence, obedience and awe, and march to a different beat, dance to an altogether different tune and live by radically different values. That's what it means to live wisely and well.

A practical application

We can see a practical application of this in the life of the missionary, Paul.

He once wrote: knowing what it is to fear the Lord, we persuade men (2 Corinthians 5 v 11). Fearing God was the impetus for his evangelism and leadership—even if it meant that everyone else regarded him as a raving idiot.

Again, this isn't cringing, petrified fear. It was reverence and awe—admiration and heart-felt appreciation that led to obedience. 'Fear the Lord' with all your heart, and telling others about him in all the glory of his death and resurrection is inevitable and irresistible.

This applies in every area of life. If we 'fear the Lord', our words will be to build up, encourage and help others to grow more like Jesus. If we 'fear the Lord' we will resist temptation because his glory and delight will be the most significant thing to us, rather than a moment of passing pleasure. If we fear the Lord we will use our resources to bless others, knowing that they are made in the image of God and that he is a just God. In every way, not least leadership, the wisdom of fearing the Lord results in living well.

Are you, as a leader, living well? Look at your relationships, your attitudes, your lifestyle, your use of money, your working pattern, the decisions you make and your motivations for making them. All of those areas are the evidence to enable you to make a sound assessment. Look at the fruit of your life in each of those areas and evaluate if it's good and desirable. Invite others into that evaluation; make it a community project. If you don't see good fruit, you can be certain it is because you fear someone or something more than the LORD.

The only response to our foolishness is repentance. Be wise: go to the cross and see how he is a God to be "feared". He is a holy and awesome God, also wise and understanding. Our willful refusal to fear him matters more than we can ever know. But for Him, our sin and the sin of the people we lead is not an insurmountable problem.

When we fear the Lord, what matters to us are his words of commendation: "Well done, good and faithful servant". When we fear the LORD, we will hate to do that which grieves Him, and love to do that which delights Him. When we fear the LORD, we will live and lead with wisdom.

 Questions for reflection

❓ Personally, what or who are you tempted to fear more than God?

❓ What truth about God speaks to that and keeps you fearing him alone?

❓ How might you evaluate whether a leader or potential leader has wisdom?

7 SERVICE

Principle

To be a leader is to be a servant.

Consider this

He sat looking at the design for quite some time. He'd never had a business card before, and he felt a little guilty about being so excited about having one!

But try as he might, he just couldn't make up his mind. Was he Pastor or Reverend? Sue, his wife, told him he should be just plain old Jon Petersen... but that was just silly, wasn't it?

Biblical background
Read Matt 23 v 1-12;
John 13 v 1-17; Acts 6:1-7

❓ What was wrong with the teachers of the Law and Pharisees' approach to leadership (Matt 23:1-7)?

❓ What alternative approach does Jesus teach and model in these passages?

❓ In Acts 6, why did the apostles choose others to wait on tables?

❓ What was the result of this decision (Acts 6:7)?

Read all about it

The constant danger facing those in leadership is a sense of their own importance. Yet if it is Jesus who still rules his church, then any form of legitimate leadership must display the mark of true humility. It will be self-effacing rather than self-promoting.

The people of God should always be self-consciously looking to live under the rule of King Jesus. In contrast, a self-promoting leader will attempt to put himself between the people of God and King Jesus. Self-regard is an attitude of heart rather than an outward expression, yet there are outward signs. Just think about the following:

Titles

C H Spurgeon said: *"Let us never court great titles nor proud degrees"*. Titles are a big issue. While there is a distinction among God's people, it ought not to be one of *office*, but of *function*. For example, given that the title "vicar" actually means "in the place of", it does not seem to be the most helpful term. Who is the vicar "in the place of?" Christ? The bishop? Some other body?

Clothing

Whether it's a dog-collar, a cassock, a suit, or the latest "cool" fashion, clothing can functionally separate you from the rest and draw attention to who you are.

Behavior

People can act as leaders in a particular way that can distinguish them from the rest of the church.

In Matthew 23 and Luke 22, Jesus identified all three of these "leadership distinctives" as wholly inappropriate. It is impossible to underestimate the occasion recorded in John 13 when Jesus washed the feet of his disciples. Don Carson notes that *"there is no instance in either Jewish or Greco-Roman sources of a superior washing the feet of an inferior."* He continues:

The reluctance of Jesus' disciples to volunteer for such a task is, to say the least, culturally understandable; their shock at his volunteering is not merely the result of being shamefaced, it is their response to finding their sense of the fitness of things shattered. But here Jesus reverses normal roles. His act of humility is as unnecessary as it is stunning, and is … a model of Christian conduct.

The matchless self-emptying of the eternal Son … reaches its climax on the cross. This does not mean that [he] exchanges the form of God for the form of a servant; it means … that he so dons our flesh … that his deity is revealed in our flesh, supremely at the moment of greatest … service.

The incarnation and the crucifixion, as modeled in the act of foot washing, reveals the kind of God he is.[6]

I suspect that no one could sustain an argument that refuted this point. To be a leader is to be a servant. The biblical teaching on the issue is clear and unambiguous. But being a servant does not simply mean washing everyone's feet! That would be too easy, inevitably becoming tokenistic — on a par with the Queen handing out gold coins to the "poor" on Maundy Thursday: a grand act of benevolence that costs the monarch very little. In contrast, here we see the act of foot-washing in the truly costly context of Jesus' imminent crucifixion.

Leadership=service

Being a servant defines leadership. It is not about any single act I perform but the overall character of my leadership. I am to exercise my leadership conscious of my duty of service to those in my care, which means that *every duty I undertake as a leader* should be done with a commitment to the good of those for whom I am responsible. Leadership says nothing about status or power. Leadership is not an opportunity for me to "get my own way". It is always about those for whom I have a responsibility of care.

---

6   D. A. Carson, The Gospel According to John (Apollos, 1991), 462

The question of hierarchy

People argue that hierarchy is simply a part of all human life, and so to say that it has no place among the people of God is an over-statement. Yet, if the Oxford English Dictionary is correct when it defines the word as *"a body of persons ... ranked in grades ... one above another"*, then we should at least challenge its appropriate-ness.

The Bible talks about oversight, and leaders are referred to as elders. This indicates that there is a legitimate and necessary distinc-tion. But as we've seen, the role of a leader is to shepherd the flock as a servant. Jesus models this radical nature of servanthood in the foot-washing incident and ultimately in the crucifixion.

This pattern of humble service is at the very center of the Christian understanding of God. Within the Trinity the Son is subservient to the Father, and the Spirit delights to do the bidding of the Father and the Son, and to give glory to Christ—but there is no corresponding view of control.

A mentor used to tell young men going into paid ministry: "You are the church's servant, but the church is not your master". That provides a helpful way of looking at this idea of service.

Yet how does a church work without hierarchy? It helps to under-stand that leaders should not have more people who are accountable to them than anyone else—and that people are not more accountable to them than they are to others. *Mutual accountability* should exist between leaders and members.

Outside of the context of God's word, a leader has no more ability or authority to tell people what to do than anyone else—**the leader has no casting vote.** Leadership is always about those for whom I have a responsibility of care. This is illustrated within the context of the family home. Male headship is not about control, it is about providing a context in which your family flourishes. Church leader-ship is about providing a context in which people flourish as the people of God and become the people God would have them be.

So servant leadership is a principle, not a strategy. It is not a ploy to get my own way. That would be manipulation and that is always wrong. Paul speaks about his rejection of underhanded methods, and the virtue of living an open life before the Corinthians (2 Corinthians 4 v 2). We need to allow this view of servanthood to shape our understanding of leadership and to permeate all our activities.

Omnicompetent?

All of this does not mean that leaders do everything! The incident in Acts 6, where the Greek-speaking widows are being overlooked in the distribution of food, is instructive.

The apostles recognize that it is an important issue, but not one for them to be personally responsible for. To "wait on table", although a good thing, was not the best thing, even though it was serving. At face value, this might seem to contradict the service model taught and modeled by Jesus: He washed their feet, yet they wouldn't even wait on tables!

But the best way for the apostles to be servants was to teach the word of God. They expended themselves on behalf of the rapidly growing congregation in prayer and preaching. The need of the widows was great, and needed an adequate response. In fact, it was *so important* that the apostles could not do it justice and also ensure that the church was taught and led well.

Their decision was strategic as much as it was principled. The reason for their refusal to wait on tables was not that it was beneath them. It was simply a matter of focus—they had to decide what was the most effective action for the community's greatest good. In other words, *it was not about them in terms of their position or status.* They were considering the people of God and the spread of the gospel. Being a servant does not always require the leader to perform every menial task.

Some leaders are so determined to be servants that they do many good but inappropriate jobs. In so doing, they do not have the best interests of the congregation at heart. They need to teach the Word, shepherd the flock and oversee the work. They can and should lead by example, which will sometimes mean sweeping the yard, vacuuming the carpet and serving the meal. But the decision to do those things must come from a prior decision that the task is truly serving God's people, and not serving my own desire to be seen as a servant. Refusing to delegate tasks can deny others the opportunity to serve. Pride can be at the root of this, too.

Self protection

Let's consider the opposite problem: some leaders, particularly of large churches, feel the need to protect themselves. It is clearly impossible for them to be personally involved in everyone's life; they cannot be at everyone's beck and call.

These leaders would be too vulnerable dishing up food in the kitchen or collecting Bibles in the church auditorium—too many people would try to talk to them; they would be overwhelmed. So they develop a system of protection by the means of people and protocol: before you can get to the leader, you have to go through a number of sub-leaders and personal assistants. Such methods of protection may seem sensible, but they need to be assessed to see where the points of conflict are with Jesus' model of leadership.

The culture we can buy into is the worldly culture of the superstar —it is about status, where everyone wants to talk to the head honcho. But in the upside-down kingdom of God, cultures are nurtured where the leaders are ordinary people, and everyone is interested in everyone else—not simply in getting a few minutes with the big guy!

As soon as it is necessary for you to become inaccessible, you need to consider carefully if you can, at the same time, remain a foot-washing servant. If you cannot hang out with the flock, are you not in danger of no longer being one of the sheep?

Service is integral to leadership, at least leadership in the upside-down kingdom of God. Keeping this perspective is easier if leaders never lose sight of the fact that they are, first and foremost, sheep!

Questions for reflection

[?] Think about church leaders that you look up to. In what ways do they show that a leader is a servant?

[?] In your church, where do you think pressure to define leadership according to worldly standards comes from:
  • The leaders' view of leadership?
  • The expectations of church members?
  • The denominational hierarchy?
  • Church tradition?
What can you do to counteract these pressures?

[?] How can you develop a servant heart in yourself?

[?] How can you encourage servant heartedness in in your church?

8 AUTHORITY

Principle

Leaders must exercise both functional and moral authority.

 Consider this

Sheila could hardly contain herself. Who did he think he was? What right did he have to speak to her like that? It was none of his business anyway.

Blood boiling, she made up her mind to speak to his wife.

Maybe the pastor's wife would see that Sheila was the one who deserved an apology, not the other way around! But then, even if she didn't see her side, Sheila was adamant that no one was going to tell her how to conduct her friendships. Or ex-friendships, in this case!

Biblical background
Read 1 Timothy 2 v 1-4; 5 v 17-20;
Ephesians 5 v 21 – 6 v 4

? What does Paul say our attitude should be towards authority in general (1 Tim 2 v 1-2)?

? What is the purpose of discipline exercised in church (1 Tim 2 v 3-4)?

? What should our attitude be towards each other (Ephesians 5 v 21 – 6 v 4)?

? What should our attitude be towards church leaders in particular (1 Tim 5 v 17-20)?

Read all about it

I may be overstating the issue a little, but I think authority in the local church is one of the most difficult areas relating to leadership. If the cultural reflection in the opening chapter is right, the society we live in makes this issue a particular problem.

Humans are suspicious of authority, and our western mindset increases that instinctive rebellion. Jim Packer put it this way:

> One tragedy of our time is that ... "authority" has become almost
> a dirty word in the Western world, while opposition to authority
> in schools, families and society generally is cheerfully accepted as
> something that is at least harmless and perhaps rather fine.[7]

Then there is the opposing problem of *leadership abuse*, where too much authority has been either assumed or granted. This in turn has further solidified our prejudices.

Our task in this chapter, therefore, is to see what the Bible says on this issue, and to ensure, as far as we are able, that our reading is not so colored by our cultural or personal preferences that we cannot sit under the authority of God's word.

So we should pause at this point for a brief reminder: we saw in earlier chapters that Christ rules his church. He has never abdicated that rule, nor is it mediated through anyone else. We see in Revelation 2 – 3 that his rule is direct and intimate. He exercises his rule by his Spirit through his word. This means that the final authority among God's people is the word of God, applied skilfully by the Spirit of God to the hearts and consciences of his people.

What authority do leaders have?

Given the repeated assertion in this book that it is Christ who rules his Church and he does so without delegation, it will be helpful if we begin with at least a working definition: **authority is the right to**

---

7   J. I. Packer, *Freedom and Authority* (Regent College, 1992), p. 11

make decisions and give direction.

Authority combines both the "right" to rule and the "might'" (apparatus) to rule. In the UK, for example, parliament, the judiciary, the police and the military all have authority by this definition. Right without might is futile, and might without right is tyranny.

In a democracy, the right of the government to rule is granted by the people. It is commonly termed a "mandate": the people give the government the mandate to rule. A law is only enforceable as long as the majority of the population observe it.

In other forms of government, the right to rule might come from the principle of succession (for example, a dynasty of emperors), but even that requires at least the people's compliance. This can be illustrated by the collapse of the Soviet Union and the totalitarian regimes of the Soviet Bloc, or even the more recent events in the Middle East. When there is a popular movement, it has the moral weight, in and of itself, to bring a government down. There comes a point at which a totalitarian government is no longer able to wield its might in order to suppress dissent.

Another example to think about is the nature of a parent's authority. It changes as the child grows into adolescence, but perhaps it always relies on an element of "permission" and co-operation. There is no doubt that co-operation is required as the boy becomes a 6-foot, testosterone-fueled, argumentative adolescent! As a parent, I soon recognized that my authority had to rely on something other than my ability to physically enforce obedience or compliance.

Functional authority

Leaders have a *functional authority* as they teach the word of God. Both publicly and from house to house, they have the responsibility to show how the gospel speaks into life and circumstances. When that is clear, the refusal to obey is ultimately a refusal to obey God.

One of the distinctive qualities of an elder is his aptitude to teach; he has to be able specifically and meaningfully to apply God's word. Not every leader is a preacher—there are many different ways of teaching the truths of the gospel. A leader has a functional authority in that he is gifted and competent as a teacher: he can demonstrate where the word applies to different problems and situations.

That is easy in issues upon which the Bible speaks unequivocally, but what about when it is implicit rather than explicit, or when there are complex cases?

Take, for example, the responsibility to love unbelievers. This is an unambiguous principle (Galatians 6 v 10), but it is not always easy to apply. Say a few of you in your Christian community have begun to befriend a woman who has a mental illness and has been begging in the street for money and cigarettes, even late at night. Clearly this makes her vulnerable. But what is the most loving course of action? Should you give her money? Should you help her manage her pension? Should you offer to accommodate her in your house?

As you discuss this question, someone in the congregation may have a different opinion to that of the leader. A leader's opinion cannot take precedence over the opinion of another simply because they are a leader. Let's make a slight detour before examining this issue further.

Default to authority

There is a biblical principle of what we might call *default to authority*. In other words, Christians should be, by conviction, submissive! We should be people whose instinct is to defer to authority: Christians to one another, wives to husbands, children to parents, employees to employers, citizens to government. We will give to Caesar what is Caesar's.

This is because anarchy is the very heart of sin: the desire to be our own god. Becoming a Christian is submitting to God-in-Christ, and then exercising that submission in relation to those to whom God calls us to submit. There is a limit on this: when obedience to man is in conflict with obedience to God, then we obey God. But that is not anarchy or self-rule; it is a humble recognition of where our ultimate loyalty lies.

It is vital in any consideration of authority to recognize that God has appointed leaders among his people. That appointment does not detract from the undelegated rule of Christ over his Church, but it is the means by which he exercises it. Again, the distinctive quality of elders in 1 Timothy 3 is their aptitude to teach, because the primary authority is the word of God.

Moral authority

But we were addressing the question of the leader's authority when biblical direction is implicit rather than explicit. In that situation, a leader's moral authority is unavoidable. This authority comes from experience and character. Elders are called elders because, at least in part, they are older. They have been around the block a few times.

But experience on its own is no teacher. These men need to have *learned* through their experience and have proved themselves through it. Because Christians are called to humility, we should humbly submit to authority, and defer to those who have proved themselves through experience and character.

The Bible has much to say about the authority of leaders:

> Now I urge you, brethren (you know the household of Stephanas, that they were the first fruits of Achaia, and that they have devoted themselves for ministry to the saints), that you also be in subjection to such men and to everyone who helps in the work and labors. I rejoice over the coming of Stephanas and Fortunatus and Achaicus, because they have supplied what was lacking on your part. For they have refreshed my spirit and yours. Therefore acknowledge such men. **1 Corinthians 16 v 15-18**

> For even if I boast somewhat further about our authority, which the Lord gave for building you up and not for destroying you, I will not be put to shame. **2 Corinthians 10 v 8**

> For this reason I am writing these things while absent, so that when

present I need not use severity, in accordance with the authority
which the Lord gave me for building up and not tearing down.

2 Corinthians 13 v 10

Nor did we seek glory from men, either from you or from others, even
though as apostles of Christ we might have asserted our authority.

1 Thessalonians 2 v 6

For you know what commandments we gave you by the authority of
the Lord Jesus. **1 Thessalonians 4 v 2**

But we request of you, brethren, that you appreciate those who dili-
gently labor among you, and have charge over you in the Lord and
give you instruction, and that you esteem them very highly in love
because of their work. Live in peace with one another.

1 Thessalonians 5 v 12-13

These things speak and exhort and reprove with all authority. Let no
one disregard you. **Titus 2 v 15**

Remember those who led you, who spoke the word of God to you;
and considering the result of their conduct, imitate their faith.

Hebrews 13 v 7

Obey your leaders and submit to them, for they keep watch over your
souls as those who will give an account. Let them do this with joy
and not with grief, for this would be unprofitable for you.

Hebrews 13 v 17

No matter how awkwardly authority sits in our cultural context,
the Bible will not permit us to throw it away. God has ordained for
leaders to lead his people. When recognized and appointed to that
task, they then have the authority to get on with it.

Questions for reflection

❓ How can we help one another in churches to welcome authority as a good gift from God?

❓ How can we avoid the abuse of authority?

❓ How can you evaluate a person's ability to exercise both functional and moral authority?

Gospel-centered leadership

9 STYLE

Principle

God made me the person I am for a reason.

Consider this

Stan walked away from the meeting with a sinking feeling in his stomach. History was repeating itself. What was it about him that caused such a reaction?

Someone had said that he was the kind of person others either loved or loathed, and that it was impossible to be neutral about him. But what could he do about it? He felt like walking away. *"Why can't people just accept me for who I am?"* he demanded of God—perhaps a little too petulantly.

Biblical background
Galatians 5 v 22-23, Ephesians 2 v 10

❓ What five words would you use to describe your leadership "style"?

❓ What does Paul say should infuse our lives and styles (Galatians 5 v 22-23)?

❓ How have you found grace refining your personal style?

❓ What has God created us for, with our particular personalities (Ephesians 2 v 10)?

Read all about it

We've been looking at aspects of leadership that are critical to distinctively biblical leadership. Like a multi-faceted gemstone set apart in its beauty, the relationship of these different aspects to each other is what makes biblical leadership distinctive.

Each aspect on its own could describe leadership in a range of situations, but I am arguing for their essential mutual dependence. Only a biblical view of leadership enables you to be a slave and genuinely lead at the same time, or calls for consensus while recognizing authority.

In this chapter we will look at the issue of style, and examine three kinds of style: gospel, cultural, and personal.

Gospel style

As evangelicals, we are ruled by King Jesus through the intimate work of the Holy Spirit as he shapes us by his word. So our distinctive leadership style should be defined by the gospel and its values. Gospel-style leadership will be servant-leadership and it will seek to lead by example. These are clear and unambiguous gospel characteristics.

The fruit of the Spirit, *"love, joy, peace, patience, kindness, goodness, faithfulness, gentleness, self-control"* (Galatians 5 v 22–23), must define our leadership style.

That list is intriguing because Paul describes these in the singular: "The **fruit** of the Spirit is…" rather than "The **fruits** of the Spirit are…". Perhaps this is because Paul's emphasis falls on the activity of the Holy Spirit, and he is the only one who can produce all nine in unison. It might be possible for us to work hard in one area — say, self-control—and make significant progress, but to develop all nine in symmetry is impossible. Only the Spirit of life can produce that kind of result, which enables leaders to be servants, to lead by the example of a transformed life, to exercise God-honoring and saint-edifying authority and to work for consensus. It is a distinctive gospel style.

So whatever the prevailing style of leadership in the world, the gospel will be that which most profoundly shapes the leadership style among the people of God. Regardless of whether I am a leader in Manchester in the 21st century, or a leader in Washington in the 19th century, or a leader in Tibet in the 16th century, there will be some similarity because the leadership style will be profoundly shaped by the gospel. The gospel is the most important aspect of leadership style; it is the bedrock.

Cultural style

It was important to begin by looking at that aspect of style which is distinctively shaped by the gospel because that is non-negotiable in any culture. However, each church setting has its own shape, texture and color—that is, it has its own distinctive culture. Leadership will to some extent—perhaps to a large extent — reflect that specific culture.

One cultural context may be more formal, and another more casual. This is not a question of right or wrong. Even though church-as-family is a biblical principle (for example 1 Timothy 3 v 5, 15), families have different ways of relating to one another. They occupy different locations on the spectrum of formality, and this is an altogether good thing!

The culture of any particular church should express the creative tension between faithfulness to the Bible and relevant engagement with the wider culture. So the cultural style of a local church, and the leadership style of that church, should be distinctive and shaped by the context.

For example, it has been suggested that the different names for church leaders in the New Testament were shaped by their cultural context: "elder" was preferred in a Jewish context, "bishop" in a Roman context, and "pastor" in a Greek context. If that is true, it probably would have shaped the particular style of leadership, too.

So if "eldership" is the prevailing model, then there will be a focus on age, status and standing. If "bishop" is the general idea of an overseer, and "pastor" carries the idea of a shepherd, then these two images would shape the style of leadership to a certain degree.

Personal style

Personal style is *"a way of behaving or approaching a situation that is characteristic of, or favored by, a particular person."*[8] It is the way you do something—the approach and manner that is distinctively you.

The theological framework for this idea is that the individuality of personal style expresses God's creativity: *"For we are God's workmanship, created in Christ Jesus for good works, which God prepared beforehand, that we should walk in them"* (Ephesians 2 v 10).

God has, by his grace, made us what we are in order to perform the tasks he has prepared for us to do. Any way in which we are good, and anything we do that is good, is a direct consequence of God's prior and creative grace. We have been re-created so that all creation will one day admire God's handiwork (see Ephesians 3 v 10). He has made each one of us individually.

I spend a lot of time talking about the corporate nature of salvation, and I am not stepping back from that. But if we talk so much about the corporate that we lose sight of the individual, we have not redressed the balance; we have just gone into another error. As 1 Peter 2 v 5 describes it, the church is made of "living stones", not mass-produced bricks! Bricks are uniform, but there is a distinctiveness about stones.

You see this individuality in creation in the distinct intricacy of a snowflake, not to mention our genetic make-up and the individuality of our fingerprints. Why am I the person I am, with my particular set of gifts and abilities? God has knit me together so that I am what I am, and grace refines me so I bring him more and more glory.

---

8   The Oxford Pocket Dictionary of Current English

Here's my observation:

Evangelicalism, as a sub-culture, defaults towards conformity and away from legitimate individual expression.

Yet Paul was not Timothy, and Barnabas was not Peter. They were all leaders in their own contexts, but their style was all their own.

Perhaps our tendency towards conformism is because we confuse godliness with niceness, and we define niceness culturally. So niceness in a middle-class English context is:

- smiling a lot
- being polite by not saying unpleasant things
- being friendly, likable, superficial, affable, bland, kind and accommodating.

"Good" leaders are then those who conform to those traits and characteristics. But this is an off-the-rack approach to leadership, and reflects a human tendency to mimic God's creation of the snowflake by making ice-cubes.

Here's my observation again: *evangelicalism, as a sub-culture, defaults towards conformity and away from legitimate individual expression.*

At the next conference you attend, have a look round the room at what people are wearing, and then glance down at the type of hand-held device they're using. Chances are you will see a whole bunch of casual shirts, chinos and iphones. Yet Paul was not Timothy, and Barnabas was not Peter. They were all leaders in their own contexts, with styles all their own.

Perhaps our tendency towards conformism is because we confuse godliness with being liked. We see influential and respected evangelical leaders and tend to conform to their characteristics—from their turns of speech right down to the style of their clothes. "Good" leaders are then those who conform to those traits and characteristics, because we can relate to them and we like them.

But we are unique individuals with a unique genetic make-up and a unique personal history because of our unique response to events.

God is sovereignly and wisely responsible for that uniqueness so that we can do the good works he has planned for us to do. I am not sure that Paul would have qualified as a leader by our middle-class criteria—he was intensely loving, but never minced his words. Many of the people we hail as evangelical heros of the past (and some of the present) are the same. They did tremendous things for the gospel but it was only these individuals who could have done them, often in conflict with the "culturally safer" evangelical church of the time. "Nicer" people perhaps would never have done the things that they were willing to do.

Those who care about being liked are often not willing to buck the trend; yet that is sometimes precisely the action required. God made the likes of these leaders to be the people he meant them to be so that, warts and all, they would do the works that God had prepared for them to do.

Of course, having our own personal style in no way justifies indulging our sin or excusing bad behavior and attitudes. But it does mean that godliness has an extensive wardrobe! In other words, the way we demonstrate love for each other will be peculiar to who we are. Love may express itself in sitting with your arms around someone as they pour out their heart to you, or it may express itself by taking a decisive course of action to solve a problem or resolve an issue.

One of the benefits in having a plurality of elders in a church is that each one can have his own style that can be appreciated and used by God to bless his people. Not all the elders have to conform to the same expression of love, though each has to be godly in the way they display the fruit of the Spirit. But they augment each other's gifts and styles, and so ensure a complementarity of styles to serve the whole church.

Conclusion

Leaders are to be soaked and marinated in the gospel. They should model the distinctiveness of the gospel in their leadership. They should also reflect and create a distinctive cultural style in their gospel community. Their own personal style should be encouraged and nurtured so as to reflect beautifully the diversity of grace. God has made us who we are with our own particular personal history so that we might make a unique contribution to this glorious thing called the church. By his power, we will each be one of those uniquely colored gemstones radiating, reflecting and glorifying God's grace, in a way that is peculiar to each one of us. Not so that people look at us and say: *"Wow!"* but so that they look at us and say: *"Isn't God glorious?"*

 Questions for reflection

- ❓ Is the gospel the foundational influence in your leadership style?

- ❓ Can you identify the cultural style of the group you lead? How well does it "express the creative tension between faithfulness to the Bible and relevant engagement with the wider culture"?

- ❓ What is your personal style? How does your personal style serve and strengthen the group you lead?

- ❓ What does your personal style lack for the nurturing of God's people? What other styles of leadership do you need to seek out and encourage to make the overall leadership of your church more rounded?

Gospel-centered leadership

10 LEADERSHIP

Principle

Leaders should lead!

Consider this

Sometimes John wanted to take a back seat and let others get on with it. But more often than not, no one did. He didn't feel comfortable with always taking the initiative; he was worried that it would make him come across as pushy, or arrogant. What could he do?

The elders had asked him to take on the conversation class for asylum seekers and refugees, and he wanted to take this responsibility seriously. He shrugged his shoulders and called the other volunteers over to give out directions.

 Biblical background
Read Titus 2

❓ What common thing is Titus told to do for all the "groups" in the church? Who is to make the first move?

❓ How is he to do this (2 v 7-8, 15)?

❓ What is the aim of this kind of leadership (2 v 5, 8, 10)?

❓ What kind of church "culture" is the result of this approach (2 v 11-14)?

❓ What does this all point to (2 v 13-14)?

Read all about it

What I am about to say is so obvious that you may think I'm actually being quite profound. Here's the thing: **being a leader is vital to leadership.** *"Leaders lead"* may appear to be a truism, but it is important to say it.

Of course, being a servant is always the defining mark of genuine Christian leadership. The primary way leaders lead is by example. But it is important in any understanding of leadership to give due weight to the need for leaders to lead **by taking the lead** among the people of God.

Jesus as a leader

The portrayal of Jesus in the four Gospel accounts show him to be a leader who takes the initiative in a dizzying range of situations. They all occur early on in the ministry of Jesus, in order to set the agenda for the kind of man and the kind of leader He is:

Matthew shows Jesus going up on a mountainside and speaking in clear and unambiguously authoritative terms (Matthew 5 – 7).

Mark records that the first public ministry tasks of Jesus were declaring the arrival of the kingdom of God and summoning four fishermen to follow him (Mark 1 v 14-20).

Luke tells of when Jesus directed Simon to put his net into the water even though the experienced fisherman had been working all night (Luke 5 v 1-11).

John relates the incident of when Jesus drove all the cattle and money lenders out of the temple, using a hastily crafted whip (John 2 v 13-17).

None of those actions undermine or contradict the servant leadership which was the defining quality of Jesus' life. All of his actions expressed his willingness to expend himself on behalf of others, and that is what it means to be a servant. He acted for God's glory and the good of others. Yet Jesus always took the lead, and was never afraid to do so. In fact, it appears that he was very determined to do so.

Paul as a leader

Likewise, Paul was not afraid to take the lead.

Paul was relatively inexperienced compared to Barnabas, who had been a follower of Jesus longer, and was the one who was first dispatched to Antioch. He took the initiative to get Saul to work with him in Antioch, and it was Barnabas and Saul whom the church in Antioch sent out at the instruction of the Holy Spirit.

Yet we discover Paul taking the lead early in their itinerant ministry (Acts 13 v 13). Paul is part of a team with whom he has close accountable relationships, but he is clearly the leader. For example, it is Paul who makes the decision about who needs to be circumcised (Acts 16 v 3) and it is Paul who dispatches Timothy and Erastus into Macedonia (Acts 19 v 21-22).

Please allow a slight digression at this point. Much is made of the need for plurality of leadership in local churches. Often the case is made from biblical examples (for example, Acts 20 v 17; 1 Timothy 5 v 17; Philippians 1 v 1; 1 Peter 5 v 1). And then common-sense arguments are brought in to show why plurality in leadership is so desirable—balancing people's weaknesses, lightening the workload, providing accountability etc—some of which were discussed in chapter 9.

However, Paul sent Titus to Crete to appoint elders (Titus 1 v 5), and Timothy to Ephesus to deal with the false teaching that had infiltrated the church (1 Timothy 1 v 3-4). The point is that, whatever plural leadership existed in Ephesus, Timothy was left to play a lead role in rectifying problems that had emerged there. Once again, none of this undermines the servant style, or the need for these men to be examples, **but lead they must.**

Nor does it mean that Paul was not a servant in that context, or that he acted in a high-handed or authoritarian way in dispatching Timothy and Erastus into Macedonia. Luke portrays Paul as being the one who takes the initiative.

Although there may be a plurality of leadership, there will often be one person—because of his experience, gifting and knowledge—who is the "first among equals". In any given leadership team, there will be someone with more experience, more maturity and more leadership skills, and it is right and appropriate that that person takes the lead.

Note that does not mean that person's will always prevails, but that the leaders should be "allowed" to lead without constant push-back and power struggles. Also, the principle of "first among equals" should apply in specific situations. So one leader on a team may have more expertise in finances, for example. He then acts as "first among equals" in that particular area.

However, plural or single leadership is not the primary issue here: whether there is one leader or five, **leaders need to lead.**

What kind of leadership do leaders give?

Direction
One of the qualifications of an elder is his aptitude to teach. If a local congregation is under the authority of Gods word (it is through the word, by the Spirit that King Jesus rules), then the elders of that congregation need to give direction to the church by setting an agenda in line with what the Bible teaches.

It isn't necessarily possible for each local church to spell out from the Bible alone the particulars of its life and ministry: there is a cultural context which will shape the specifics. But the word of God needs to be central in every congregation because God rules by his word.

How the word is taught will be determined to some extent by the surrounding context: monolog preaching, dialog teaching, gospel conversations around the kitchen table, or a comforting two-second reminder that God is sovereign might all be ways to proclaim God's word. Every church must be committed to getting the gospel out, but how it does that will be determined by the context. Leaders set the agenda by teaching the word of God, but they also need to read their culture in order to direct God's people in their particular context.

Leaders are to be neither merely responsive nor passive. They are to set the lead under the gospel. That is clearly what Paul wanted

Timothy and Titus to do in Ephesus and Crete, respectively. There were issues to be resolved in both situations. Paul was not merely concerned with the small details of church order (which is often the mistaken reading of these letters)—rather, he wanted these men to set a gospel agenda, giving direction to those churches.

We have already seen how leadership reflects the surrounding culture. One of the issues in the western world is the prevailing view of individual autonomy and a corresponding cynicism about leadership. This in part has led to arguments for "flat structures" of leadership—where everyone has an equal say—or flat structures in general, sometimes to the extent that leaders become functionally nonexistent within a church.

The impact of this has "neutered" a lot of leaders. Any kind of leadership is seen as dictatorial. We have already seen that God is the Leader above all others, and King Jesus actively rules his church. Human leadership, in whatever way it is exercised, operates under that leadership and is intended to point to and model that leadership. God leads by giving direction. Leaders are to provide direction insofar as they direct people in a manner consistent with God's agenda.

Culture creation

Part of setting direction is developing a culture. In a sense, culture-creation encapsulates what leaders need to do: it is by far the most important responsibility of leaders.

Every group, whatever its size or demographic, will naturally create its own culture within a short space of time. Those within the group will have a certain way of doing things and a certain way of relating to each other. They will have a certain outlook and set of expectations. Someone within the group, or one group within a larger group, will be particularly influential in that process of culture-creation. They will do that through the strength of their character or their quiet influence. Sometimes someone *not* saying something influences us.

An existing group will change its culture depending on the characters who come in. Leaders should therefore take the lead in creating a particular culture. If the leader isn't setting the culture, he is not the "leader"—regardless of his title. Leaders need to know:

- what kind of culture they want to create.
- what kind of relationships they want to see develop.
- what kind of priorities they want to see people take on board.
- what kind of expectations people are going to have of one another.

That culture will be created through prayer, Bible teaching, example and influence.

Timothy and Titus were given the task of creating a gospel culture in Ephesus and Crete. This would grow out of the way that they dealt with wrong beliefs and wrong behavior. Problems arose in Crete and particularly Ephesus because of a lack of a gospel culture.

False teachers were going from house to house, funded by wealthy widows. Things were allowed to go on that were neither right nor godly (Titus 1 v 10–11; 2 Timothy 3 v 6–7).

The same thing happened in Corinth. The surrounding culture had been carried wholesale into the culture of the churches (for example, 2 Corinthians 11 v 1–15). What leaders need to do is create a gospel culture which will, always and at some point, be at odds with the surrounding culture. The way that people outside the church relate to each other will not be the same as the way in which those within the church relate to each other.

The ambitions and expectations of those outside the church will differ from those within the church: the gospel will shape those in the church instead of the tyranny of self. Leaders need to take the lead in forming that gospel culture; it is not something that will happen naturally or inevitably.

This gospel culture not only needs to be created, but also sustained. A culture needs to be created where it is normal to know *what the gospel has accomplished* (the indicatives), and consequently *how we are to live* (the imperatives); a culture where where people are constantly reminded of who they are in Christ. We need to remind one another of the essential truths of the gospel: that we are more sinful than we dare admit and more loved than we would ever dare believe. All the *imperatives* of the gospel (what we are to do) will flow out of these *indicatives* (what the gospel has accomplished). We will therefore forgive one another because we are forgiven much. We will want to be holy because we have been made in the image of God to be holy. These truths about who we are in Christ are going to be the main means by which leaders can shape a culture.

This is an important issue because our surrounding culture fights to shape and define us. If the gospel is the defining feature of a group, then people are pastored more easily and pointed to Jesus more effectively. Problems become more acute when anything other than the gospel is the defining feature.

Initiative

If leaders are going to set the direction and create a culture, they need to be the people who take the initiative. They have to take the initiative by getting involved in people's lives, by teaching them, and speaking to them gently about the gospel in order that the gospel imperatives are obeyed instinctively and faithfully.

When that is not happening, leaders need to be prepared to take the initiative and "eyeball" somebody by telling them that they are not living consistently with the gospel. Leaders need to be prepared to pick people up on both behavior and belief. It means being prepared to stand up to people who have an unhealthy influence on a group.

Paul says to Timothy that it is not simply about teaching truth but also about refuting error (2 Timothy 4 v 1–4). Leaders have to take the responsibility of refuting error. What the Bible implies, and history demonstrates, is that people want some kind of lead; people will be led. We labor under the myth of our own autonomy. Our autonomy is expressed in the person whom we allow to lead us. Leaders need to make sure that they take the initiative to lead in a good and godly direction.

Failure to lead

There are several reasons why leaders do not take the lead in direction, culture creation or initiative. One reason is the refusal to take responsibility, and the principle reason for this is idolatry. That idolatry expresses itself in a number of ways:

- **Our own comfort** means that we do not always want to expend our energy in giving direction, in creating a culture or in taking the initiative.
- **Our need to be liked** is also a form of idolatry. We choose not to confront someone because we want them to like us, when the most loving thing to do would be to challenge them about a certain attitude or behavior.
- Another danger is **reputation**. Prominent leaders may wish to build their church in terms of numbers so that they have a reputation of having increased a congregation from 20 to 100. Having built that reputation they don't want to risk losing people—and so losing the name they have built for themselves —and so they avoid conflict.

Another reason for refusing to take responsibility to lead is apathy. Apathy is an absence of affection, emotion or feeling. It is a terrible thing when leaders have no real affection for God or his people. We must care if someone has stopped being part of the church or started to go out with a non-Christian or has got a job on the other side of the country. Some leaders simply do not care enough to do anything about these matters. Leaders need to be people with a passion for God and his church. When that passion is absent, perhaps our heart has grown cold because it is growing hard.

Questions for reflection

? Examine the culture of your church community. Are there aspects of that culture which need to come under the sound of the gospel? What concrete steps need to take place for this to happen?

? Are there aspects of your church's life where you can take initiative to serve Jesus in new ways and encourage others to do the same?

? Think about the reasons given for a failure to step up to proactive leadership—comfort, being liked, reputation and apathy. Which of these is your greatest danger? What false thinking do you listen to which legitimizes these approaches?

Gospel-centered leadership

PART THREE
PRACTICALITIES

11 DECISIONS! DECISIONS!

Principle

Decision making in the local church should be about seeking a Spirit-inspired consensus.

Consider this

"Should we choose carpet or laminate for the new floor?"
"What font should we use on the service sheet?"
"Can the singers rehearse on Thursday instead of Monday?"

"If I have to deal with one more fiddly little question I will explode!" thought Phil. These mundane details seemed such a distraction from the real business of teaching the gospel. When did his role as church leader turn into administration?

His church was in the process of making a big decision and he was beginning to believe that dictatorship was a great idea. Why couldn't everyone see the benefits of the change? Despite his frustration, Phil knew that working for consensus was the right way to come to any decision—even if it meant the change that he was hoping for and praying for didn't go forward.

Biblical background
Read 1 Corinthians 10 v 31-11 v 1

? What is Paul's "rule of thumb" when it comes to deciding what to do (10 v 31)?

? What is the result of this approach (10 v 32-33)?

? How does this impact our view of the "mundane"?

? How does this approach point people to Jesus (11 v 1)?

Read all about it

Imagine this scenario: the leadership proposes that the congregation should devolve into five small, geographically-located and missionally-focused gospel communities. Everyone will be required to be in one of these gospel communities. Most church activities will then take place in those communities—prayer, Bible study, discipleship, evangelism, relationships, baptism—leaving the whole church with just one time per week where they all gather to sing together and hear the Bible taught.

This appears to be a big decision, and not one the leadership should impose upon the congregation, not least because it requires an active buy-in. But there are good gospel reasons for adopting this strategy. For example:

- **Mission:** relationships work better in smaller groups; each of the gospel communities can have a particular mission focus.
- **Diversity:** different styles across the communities means a wider range of things can be done.
- **Location:** it enables the gospel to get into the nooks and crannies of local sub cultures.

One of the leaders makes the proposal and highlights the reasoning behind the developments. There is a lot of discussion and a number of questions, mainly about the practicalities of the arrangement. The church is then asked to talk it over together and pray about it for a month, after which time the church will reconvene and make the decision. Most people are persuaded and happy to adopt the strategy, but a small handful of people are not yet on board.

What do you do?
- *Push it through because the leaders are convinced that this is the way forward?*
- *Take a vote and be satisfied with an 85% majority?*
- *Throw out the idea?*
- *Shelve it until next year?*

There's a lot of misunderstanding about consensus, and some see it as incompatible with leadership. Functionally, consensus can mean lead to the tyranny of the minority, because a decision can be thwarted by the non-compliance of just one person!

Consensus is the decision-making process that requires full agreement before final action. The benefit of that definition is that the emphasis is upon the process as much as it is upon the outcome. However, I think the definition needs to go further:

Consensus is decision-making that requires full agreement before final action; it is reliant upon the work of the Holy Spirit in his church, and intentionally uses the process as a means of discipleship and mission.

We'll look at two distinctive elements of consensus decision making: reliance and intentionality.

1. Reliance

There is something inherently risky about consensus. The notion of depending upon full agreement before final action seems a "nice-theory-shame-about-the-practice" kind of idea! Tying yourself down to this approach is something of an act of faith. I am not being super-spiritual. It is clear that when you have a diverse and unpredictable group of people together, you have the constant threat of inertia or meltdown. In that situation you have three options of final resort: management techniques, despair, or prayer.

But it is right and good for us to be dependent upon God's Spirit in our leadership. The New Testament describes Christians as the people of God "come of age" (see 1 Corinthians 14 v 20; Galatians 3, especially verses 4–5, 23–27). *We are not children anymore.*

Paul's whole argument with the believers in Corinth was that they were acting as if they were still children. The gospel, applied by the Holy Spirit to new hearts, meant that they had all that they needed for life and godliness. They were lacking nothing necessary to be mature and confident believers. We are sons of God, indwelt by the

Spirit of wisdom and understanding, who are called to have transformed minds so that we can prove what the will of God is (Romans 12 v 1-3). When that is the raw material, it seems that you have the ideal circumstances and conditions for consensus leadership genuinely to work.

God calls us to trust him and we do that as we trust his work in his people. It is his church and he promises to build it. It is extraordinary that at the close of 2 Corinthians, where Paul has had to face serious threats to the gospel, he leaves the troublesome church in the hands of God (2 Corinthians 13 v 1-7). Paul's confidence is in the power of God to be at work in his people.

Finally, when the church in Jerusalem was facing an issue with global implications, they met to discuss the Gentile affair. After much discussion, this is what they said:

> "It seemed good to the apostles and the elders, with the whole church
> ... It seemed good to us, having become of one mind ... for it seemed
> good to the Holy Spirit and to us." **Acts 15 v 22-29**

We do not know the specifics of the process, but what we do know is that Luke is presenting it as being the decision of the whole company. There was unanimity, and a commonality of conviction brought about by the Holy Spirit doing his abundant work of grace among his people.

This was a supernatural decision with potentially huge prejudice and other cultural forces working against it. There was already a precedent for this process in Acts 6 with the issue of the neglected widows. Once again, it was a hugely significant issue and the apostles gave direction, but they did so with confidence in the people of God (Acts 6 v 3-6). It might appear a risky strategy, and it can be fraught with tension, but the alternatives seem far less appealing.

2. Intentionality

It's important to approach this process with a clear and stated intention. This is not simply a leadership technique; it is a gospel tool—and a sharp and effective tool at that! Here is the assertion:

Consensus decision-making is to be adopted as an intentional strategy because it exposes heart issues to the light of the gospel in a way that no other decision-making process does. Any other method avoids vital heart issues that should be exposed in the decision-making process.

Take the scenario we began with. Consensus requires that you do not proceed with the proposal. The people who are hesitant need to be honored and listened to. You also need to be aware that the Holy Spirit may in fact be leading you as a church through their hesitancy. You then go and speak to each of the "dissenters" and talk through their doubts and questions. At some point in the process, the nature of their objections will become clear, and you will be able to discern the heart issues and respond accordingly. There are positive and helpful possibilities:

- **Concern for others.** There may be a concern for people on the fringes who may be unsettled by the changes. This is a right concern.
- **Strategy.** There may be people who are not persuaded by the strategy, believing that it will dissipate the resources of the church. There may be those who believe too much change has taken place recently and instead of going with the proposed strategy, they would like to see resources pooled instead.
- **Diversion.** There are those who may believe that the church will become so consumed with setting up these gospel communities that, ironically, their eyes are taken off mission.

Leaders need to listen to the above arguments, as they are legitimate concerns. It may be, in the end, that they are not compelling reasons against making the changes, but it is vital to listen to them and take them on board for the sake of God's glory.

But there are also less encouraging possibilities for the hesitancy:

- **Control.** People do not like change and do not want to see it happen. This process helps expose such people's reactions.
- **Security.** People find security in their structures and so are fearful of doing things differently. This is a heart issue that needs addressing with the gospel.
- **Comfort.** People find change draining and like the way things are done. Again this consensus approach to decision-making exposes people's hearts.

Notice that each of these reasons reflects a heart that has not been captured by the gospel or softened by the Holy Spirit.

Assertive, directive leadership would not have exposed those issues and people would have been left unpastored. Defaulting to the majority would not have exposed those issues either. Both of those alternative strategies may well have enabled you to move forward faster, but neither will have given you the opportunity to bring the gospel to bear on the recesses of a believer's heart and so see real change.

Nor should we underestimate the evangelistic significance of submitting to this process. It will commend the gospel in ways that a sermon never could. If non-Christians witness a room full of people engaging with an issue with due seriousness, mutual affection, appropriate honor and a defining love for God and his glory, they will see something truly supernatural. We need to disciple the people of God so that they engage with an issue and each other in that way, conscious of the gospel benefit of the approach.

Discipline

Consensus is a God-honoring way to lead a church. It allows God to lead his church. It requires us to rely on the Holy Spirit and trust his work among his people. It requires us to be proactive and to take seriously our responsibility to pastor the church intentionally.

I have used this method in a range of situations for the last 25 years. There have been times when I have been tempted to adopt an alternative approach, but I remain convinced of its value and benefit.

Discipline is an indispensable element of discipleship. If someone is continually setting their mind and heart against the leadership and others in a way that is unhelpful, then it gives leaders an opportunity to keep pursuing those issues and to bring that person to the point of discipline.

The purpose of discipline is always restorative (1 Corinthians 5 v 1–5). The problem is often that leaders do not go the full way with discipline because they do not believe it can restore people. There is an unspoken fear that discipline will not work, but it is God's way of shepherding people. Think of the prodigal son in Luke 15. The father was not abdicating his responsibility when he gave his son his inheritance; it was the father's strategy to bring the son to his senses. Even if it results in excommunication, discipline is what is needed to bring someone to his or her senses. Consensus leadership exposes aspects of hard hearts. In this way, the gospel may be brought to bear more efficiently than is possible with other means.

So what happens when one person is unwilling to shift on their opinion despite everybody else being in agreement? A leader needs to look at and address what is going on in this person's heart. Leaders need to be skilful shepherds of God's people. They need to talk with these people, invest in them and approach them both as a brother and as an under-shepherd.

At some point, a leader may need to question this person's thinking. Perhaps they believe that God is leading them in one direction, while the rest of the congregation believe God is leading them in another. It is almost guaranteed that this will not be the only issue in this person's life. If time is taken to pastor this person, then the other issues that need addressing will be raised.

Nominalism

But how would this style of leadership work in large established churches with a high percentage of nominal Christians? It works in that situation because it demonstrates the need for conversion. A church that is made up of non-Christians is a contradiction. The only two options for someone in leadership in this kind of church is to either get the people converted or get the people out. The church will not be built otherwise. A leader in consensus decision-making is able to expose issues boldly. They seek deliberately to persuade the congregation to go in a certain direction. If they are unable to persuade people, then a leader should pursue the reasons for that. Consensus leadership is used to expose heart issues and bring the gospel to bear, whether that is in a church of believers or a "church" of unbelievers.

Objections

It is fair to say that consensus decision-making is not often well regarded. I have heard various objections raised, including:

- *"It sounds good in theory, but it doesn't work in the real world."*
- *"It's too democratic, so leaders can't lead."*
- *"The group can be hijacked by a small number of people, which slows everything down."*
- *"It's impractical to consult with a group of more than about 30 people."*
- *"I haven't seen any working examples, and anything that I've seen that vaguely approaches it has been a basket-case."*
- *"I'm looking to church-plant out of an existing congregation of 180. Surely I'm not expected to get consensus at every point."*

It is beyond the scope of this chapter to address all these objections in detail, much less to dismiss them with a glib response. Perhaps the best way to approach them is to clear away some misunderstanding about the nature, practice and scope of consensus.

Not every single individual is involved in every single decision. For example, the whole of the church in Antioch was not involved in the decision to send Barnabas and Saul. From Acts 13 v 1-5 it seems that only the leadership of the church was responsible for the decision, but there was consensus among the "prophets and teachers".

It is right and effective for different groups in a church to be responsible for making certain decisions. For example, some eldership "boards" operate with an "executive" (a selected group from among the elders), who are given the authority, and responsibility to make certain day-to-day decisions. The wider eldership hold the executive accountable, but the executive have the freedom to get on and make decisions.

This works best with a process of "retrospective assessment"— that is, there is freedom for people to make decisions, but always with the understanding that their decisions could be questioned after the event if the other elders were not in agreement. This affords both freedom and accountability in which the decisions and actions are evaluated.

It is possible for the wider church to operate in this way also. For example, a leadership team took the decision to scrap an old grand piano for an electronic keyboard. Financially, it was a sensible decision because the piano needed extensive work, but a number of the congregation questioned the wisdom, not least on missional grounds! They wanted to raise the money specifically for the purchase of a replacement piano, arguing that it created a better atmosphere for non-Christians who came to gatherings.

The leadership listened to the advice and conceded the point. The whole process was conducted in a godly way. The people concerned had the freedom to question the leadership, but the challenge was humble and respectful.

Finally, if consensus decision-making is an effective discipleship tool, is there not the imagination to create structures to facilitate it, whatever the size of the church? For example, devolve the majority of church life (eg: discipleship, mission, pastoral care, communion, baptism) into smaller communities. Here significant decisions affecting the life of the small group can be discussed and worked through by consensus.

The groups can also work through any questions relating to the "combined church", which the combined leadership then acts on.

Summary

Consensus leadership is not a process by which the leadership get what they want. It is a process that shapes the life of the whole church. It is important for a leader to open up an issue for wide-ranging discussion, as it allows the Spirit of God to be at work in the people of God to shape what the church looks like.

A leader needs to work hard at culture creation so that there is no sense of fear or manipulation and that people are prepared to contradict a leader. A leader is to live their life openly before the congregation so that church members can hold a leader accountable and rebuke them. If people are prepared to rebuke a leader, then they will not be easily manipulated. 2 Corinthians 4 v 1-2 shows how this was precisely Paul's approach to local church ministry:

> Therefore, since we have this ministry, as we received mercy, we do not lose heart, but we have renounced the things hidden because of shame, not walking in craftiness or adulterating the word of God, but by the manifestation of truth commending ourselves to every man's conscience in the sight of God.

Questions for reflection

? Think about the last major decision that your church made as a whole. How did it work? Were there "winners" and "losers"?

? What would you find most difficult about adopting a consensus approach to church decision-making?

? What "heart issues" might such a process expose in you?

12 WHEN IT ALL GOES WRONG

Principle

Idealism is the enemy of gospel ministry

Consider this

Ian put down the phone with a sigh. He slumped back in his chair and tried to figure out how he would inform the rest of the church that one of their elders had left his family and run off with a neighbor, turning his back on the gospel. A broken family, broken relationships, broken trust... how could he begin to care for these people in the messy aftermath of this heartbreaking situation?

James held his head in his hands. What was he doing? He felt the weight of responsibility, but simply wanted to jump on a plane and escape to some place far away. He couldn't stomach facing the other leaders and confessing his struggle. Maybe he should just leave...

Biblical background
Read 2 Corinthians 13 v 1-14

❓ What was the church in Corinth like (see 2 Corinthians 11)?

❓ How does Paul seek to deal with this (13 v 2, 10-11)?

❓ How does Paul view himself in the face of these problematic Christians (13 v 4, 9)?

❓ What is his attitude towards the Corinthians (13 v 4, 7, 9-10)?

❓ To whom does he ultimately entrust these believers (13 v 7, 9, 14)?

Read all about it

Idealism is the enemy of relationships of all kinds, and something that Christians seem especially prone to.

At one level it is understandable. We serve a God who is perfect, who is creating a new community in Christ that reveals his glory to the world. He has put his Spirit in our hearts to help us grow more like Christ, and to love one another as Jesus loved us. Shouldn't we expect church to be brilliant?

Well, *yes and no.*

Many of the letters in the New Testament were written into situations where things had gone "pear shaped"[9] in one way or another. If it wasn't the gross immorality of Corinth, it was the abandonment of the gospel in Galatia. Even if there was no direct problem being addressed, there are warnings lurking in the background of every letter about very real dangers that individuals and whole churches were vulnerable to.

Idealism is the enemy of the gospel, because it doesn't take into account the truth that churches and Christians live in two worlds —the perfect world to come, and the failing sin-ridden world that is passing away. Idealism is where we create a fantasy dream-world where the church is perfect, and everyone lives happily ever after. We think we are encapsulating a biblical vision for the church. But then it enslaves us. We can't cope with anything less than perfection, and it doesn't take seriously the fact that people are sinful and weak.

It is a dream shared by Christian leaders and congregations alike that is just waiting to be turned into a nightmare. And the point at which this happens is the meat and drink of tabloid newspapers. *"Vicar runs off with organist's wife" "Church treasurer steals building fund!" "Youth worker is a paedophile!"*

Our leadership is tested under moments of pressure—when God's people don't behave as they ought, or when we don't behave as we ought.

---

9   Pear shaped is a peculiar British expression used to describe things that have gone disastrously wrong: "It's all gone pear shaped!"

Here are some common reactions that congregations and ministers make to such disasters that you may recognize:

- **Despairing.** Someone you trusted has failed publicly and cata-strophically. Perhaps there had been warning signs that you ignored. Perhaps it was out of the blue. You and everyone else are upset by the mess. Grieved for the sinner. Shocked at the betrayal, and your foolishness at having been taken in for so long. Embarrassed to be in the spotlight and looking so stupid. Despair reaches into your heart and you just want to give up. You lose all sense of perspective on the situation.

- **Echoing.** Many Christian leaders are so dumbstruck by disaster, all they are able to do is echo what everyone else says: *"Isn't it terrible"*. *"How could he have done that?"* *"How could she have fooled us for so long?"* You are in a state of virtual paralysis—unable to make any sensible contribution to what is happening, except by empathizing with the grief of others.

- **Assassinating.** This is a common way of protecting your idealized dream of what you think church ought to be, but is not. By making the perpetrator into an enemy. By slandering them and assassinating their character, you are able to preserve your false belief in an "ideal" church.

While understandable at some level, all three of these responses represent an abandonment of our gospel-centered ministry respon-sibilities. When the shepherd has proved to be false and has abandoned them, or when the wolves of false teaching are free in the field, this is the moment when the flock is at its most vulner-able. It is the moment when the church most needs to hear the voice of the Good Shepherd. It is the moment when the true leader will respond very differently, because he has not been taken in by the idol of idealism.

He has read his Bible. He knows the names Judas and Demas. He has read Paul saying at the end of his life: *"Everyone has abandoned me."* He can say with Robert Murray McCheynne: *"I know that within me lies the seed of every known sin"*. Shocked and saddened he may be, but he is not, deep down, surprised.

What is astonishing in the New Testament is the way Paul writes to troubled and wayward churches in prayerful hope of restoration, rather than with resigned abandonment. It strikes me that few of us Christian leaders today would be able to cope with a church like those in Corinth or Galatia. I grew up among Christians concerned with issues of church purity who talked at great length about second-degree separation. I doubt they would have given churches like Corinth or Galatia a second thought. They would have been abandoned and despised as cast-offs.

Applying the gospel

This is the point where you test your character and competency as a leader. Insightfully, persuasively and courageously applying the gospel to that situation means that, instead of the "natural" reactions above, you respond like this:

- **Not despairing.** Because you know that we live in a fallen world, and you know that God rules. Failure and scandal may be catastrophic for a particular local church and destroy it completely, or set back its work for years. But it can *never* be a failure for the gospel or of God's sovereign purposes.
- **Not echoing.** You are a leader because of your experience and gifting. You have a responsibility to shepherd the flock at the moment when they are most exposed. You must be proactive to protect them. You must bring the light of the gospel to bear on the situation. Sometimes this will mean uncovering the real issue beneath the presenting issue. In the church in Galatia the heated arguments were all about circumcision. Paul refuses to be drawn and remains neutral on the subject, saying: *"For in Christ Jesus neither circumcision nor uncircumcision counts for anything, but only faith working through love."* (Gal 5 v 6). Instead he focuses on the central issue of the gospel with clarity and passion.

- **Not assassinating.** You need to stop the flock from being ravaged by self-righteous despair. If people have been betrayed by a gifted leader, and had their confidence shattered, they need help. They need to know that he was not their savior. They need to have their eyes turned to the true Savior.

I have experienced the pain of these kinds of traumatic events more than once in my ministry so far, and expect them to happen again. When I thought of myself as a leader in God's place, I invariably handled it badly. When I thought it was my church, I fell apart. But when I finally understood it was God's church, I fell to my knees.

One of the congregations I was involved with a few years ago was led by a gifted man. He had seen the church grow and a large number of keen young people had been won for Christ through his ministry. Disaster struck one day, and he abandoned his congregation, his faith and his Christian friendships, leaving behind a devastated group of people. Me included.

Rather than wallow in despair, we organized a meeting with the whole congregation. We allowed people to express their frustrations and sadness, and to ask their many questions. We prayed for him and for ourselves. We prayed for grace and wisdom. We gave it some time to sink in, and gave ourselves as leaders to visiting pastorally each member of the congregation to talk and pray. We addressed the issue head on with careful, responsible shepherding that brought the light and hope of the gospel into a bleak situation, and by God's grace held on to everyone.

But what about you?

I am conscious as I write this that not all disasters are those that happen to others. The New Testament gives us no grounds for thinking that the catastrophe of apostasy or immorality is not going to happen time after time after time. And it has enough warnings for us to realize that it could easily be me— or you.

One of the biggest enemies of gospel ministry is idealism. And when that idealism is crushed and your heart broken, it will turn you into a cynic. The way to get round it is to repent of idealism.

But idealism isn't the problem of just the minister. Congregations suffer from it too.

There should be a healthy respect for those in leadership. Scripture tells us that we mustn't muzzle the ox and that we are to share all good things with those who teach us. But healthy respect can easily turn into people idealizing you and placing you on a pedestal. A state of affairs that many leaders are happy to live with because it strokes their egos.

But when the leader's flaws are revealed and they come crashing down, all the congregation is left with is shattered dreams and a cynical disgust of all things Christian. Idealism also crushes the people for whom I am responsible.

The gospel antidote to this common state of affairs is clear. It starts with recognizing that **you are not Jesus!** You cannot save them. You are not even their leader. Only Christ is. Make sure that you recognize the signs of how this false thinking starts and establishes itself, and be quick to put a stop to it—in others as well as yourself.

Questions for reflection

❓ What might some of the signs be that a person or congregation is idealistic in an unhealthy way?

❓ How could you be unconsciously fuelling these wrong thoughts?

❓ Which of the three reactions are you most prone to: despairing, echoing or assassinating? What does this tell you about your heart?

❓ How can you prepare your church for a disaster that must inevitably come? What elements do you need to include in your preaching and conversation to make sure that no one is unrealistically idealistic?

❓ What are the "triggers" that put you in a place where you are prone to falling down yourself? How can you recognize the signs of vulnerability? What can you do to protect yourself and your congregation from your failings?

Ideas for action

❓ Countries and businesses expend a lot of effort on "Disaster planning". Does your church have a disaster plan?

❓ Meet with your leadership team and think through the various likely scenarios that might arise. Talk about what you might do in each situation not just to minimize the damage, but to encourage gospel growth.

Gospel-centered leadership

13 LETTING HIS PEOPLE GROW

Principle

Leaders exist to serve others intentionally, to help them grow and mature in Christ.

Consider this

Paul was a little bit nervous about handing over the sermon to Dan. Would he be able to teach the passage and engage their church in the application? Was he ready for this task?

Teaching God's word was serious business, and needed to be done well. But Dan had good Bible knowledge and a heart for the Lord, and was a gifted speaker. He had to start somewhere!

Biblical background
Hebrews 12 v 5-11, 1 Peter 5 v 1-4

🔲 How does God show his love for his children (12 v 6)?

🔲 What is his aim (12 v 10-11)?

🔲 How does Peter describe an elder's role (5 v 2)?

🔲 How does he describe Jesus' role (5 v 4)?

🔲 What can we conclude about God's involvement with his people from these passages?

🔲 How does that change the way we should lead (see. 5 v 2-3)?

Read all about it

Intentionality. It is a key word when thinking about leadership. Intentional in our relationships. Intentional in our conversations. Intentional in our use of time. Intentional in our ambitions for others.

Leadership that lacks intentionality lacks purpose, direction and influence. It's leadership that leads nowhere.

Leaders need to recognize that the aim of leadership is the growth and development of the people for whom we are responsible. They are not there to serve my perceived needs, eg: affirmation, identity or purpose. But it is equally as important to realize that neither am I there as a leader to serve their perceived needs.

Leaders are there to serve others intentionally with a view to their godliness and maturation.

That's the point Paul is making in Ephesians 4. The leadership roles he cites are there to to *"equip the saints for works of service for the building up of the body of Christ ... to mature manhood, to the measure of the stature of the fulness of Christ" (v 12-14)*.

All this is so that we will be equipped to "gospel one another" (v 15, *"speaking the truth in love"*)—so that we function together as that for which the Lord made us.

Paul then goes on to describe the characteristics of the (dis)communities of darkness out of which they came, and the communities of light which they now are. As those communities of light, they are the means by which the darkness is not only dispelled, but more significantly transformed, as sinners turn to the light and submit to Christ (5 v 13-14).

This objective needs to be in view as we lead with intentionality. Ministry is not done by a select few, the elite, the professionals. Gospel ministry is the call of God on the life of every believer, and gospel witness is the purpose of every church.

Leaders need to lead with that end in view, and that purpose shaping their activity. We might call this, **leading in reverse**. We know what we want to achieve, so we work back from that in such a way as best helps that end point to be accomplished.

So if our purpose is equipping God's people for works of ministry because that is how they as individuals and the body as a whole grows, how will it shape my current activity?

1. I won't do everything!

People in leadership tend to be competent people. Generally, that's a good thing. Incompetent leaders would be (and are!) a real nightmare. However, competency can lead to delusions of grandeur, and perhaps the only thing worse than an incompetent leader is one who thinks of him or herself as competent at everything. So one of the reasons I won't do everything is for the simple reason *that I can't do everything.* At least there will be things others can do better than I. Leadership is, in part, having the humility to recognize that, and so allowing and encouraging others to do them.

But it also means that *I resist the temptation to do things*—even if I actually am able to do them better than others. Competency is not something that comes out in full bloom. It takes time to develop and nurture. If leadership is about helping other flourish and thrive as they use their gifts for God's glory and the good of others, then as a leader it is my responsibility to give them tasks and release them into ministry. This is the principal way they will grow into maturity. Of course they will make mistakes, but each time they do is a moment of opportunity for grace and growth.

2. I will invest in people

Just as a good marriage is the best context for children to learn what a good marriage looks like, good leaders grow good leaders. Good leaders do not see others as mere commodities to serve their ambitions but as sheep in their care, and as gospel ministers they have a responsibility to nurture.

That means I will invest in people by spending time with them, sharing my life with them, teaching them along the way and in the moment. I will be beside them in times of joy and sorrow, failure and success, disappointment and satisfaction. I will take these "moments" and view them as opportunities for grace by shining the light of the gospel upon them. I cannot do that if I am detached from people, cocooned in my study or indifferent to their mundane lives and their many questions and predicaments.

3. I won't be content with running programs

Programs are easy to plan and run. People are anything but! Which is why so many of us are good at running programs, putting together series, preparing sermons and Bible studies. For some, there is no greater pleasure than spending a couple of days at the end of the year planning what the next 12 months are going to look like in terms of the issues being addressed, the material being developed and the sexy titles that will grab attention.

Please hear me on this: this is not all bad. In fact, it can be very good. But I can *never* be content with that in the sense that I use those things as a measure of my ministry. The measure of our ministry as leaders is the people we lead. Are they "growing in grace and in the knowledge of the Lord Jesus"? It is a common question after a sermon to ask the preacher how it went. To which the correct answer is: "We'll have to wait and see". Our ministry is not judged by one talk, and a sermon is not judged in the moment. A fruitful ministry is growth in the godliness of the people among whom I am ministering.

4. I will ensure my teaching and mentoring are tailored

Gospel ministry worthy of that name can never be a "one-size-fits-all" approach. Bible teaching is often, out of necessity, general because it is addressing groups of individuals, each one with their own circumstances.

When Paul was writing his letters, he would not have known every person who was listening to them being read, and yet he brought gospel truth to bear on their situation. But it was important that each congregation had elders who were "apt to teach", that is, to show how the truth of God's word is relevant to the lives of the individuals in their care.

Bible teaching from the front on a weekly basis is, in and of itself, inadequate to grow a congregation. It can and should set the agenda, but it needs to be taken and massaged deep into the hearts of our people. Without that we will have a tendency to breed hearers and critics, men and women with big heads but small hearts.

5. I won't be content with numbers

Numbers are a massive distraction for all of us in ministry, and the most frequent means of self deception. It works both ways. If leaders have a numerically growing church, they tend to congratulate themselves on their gospel impact. If we have stagnated numerically or even shrunk, we tend to congratulate ourselves on our gospel faithfulness.

But numbers, in and of themselves, signify nothing. There are many church buildings that are packed week by week with people listening to a preacher who preaches a false gospel of health and prosperity. Do those numbers validate that ministry? *Of course not.* So how can numbers they validate the ministry of those who do preach the gospel?

Disciples are what validates our leadership. Men and women who grow in their love of Christ and their devotion to Him. People who allow the gospel to shape their decisions about where they live, who they marry, whether they marry, what jobs they do and what kind of spouse they are. Large numbers merely give leaders a greater opportunity to nurture disciples. If we fail to do that, we are squandering a God-given resource for the sake of our own ego.

6. I will build structures with people at the center

If all the above is true, this final piece of the jigsaw is as inevitable as it is necessary. Leaders need to build structures that will best encourage and facilitate the growth of those in our care.

If a weekly Sunday sermon is an inadequate diet for growing a Christian or congregation, then leaders need to build structures where that word can be applied and worked out throughout the week. Leaders need to train other leaders who can skillfully, courageously, gently and persuasively take the taught word and massage it into hearts and lives. The structures we build will serve this end.

So, for example, *we will not build structures that exclusively center around one particular leader* but devolve power and responsibility to others. We might call these home groups, cell groups, missional communities, city groups, life groups or gospel communities. The name is irrelevant; the purpose and function is what matters. They need to be groups of people who not only do Bible study together but learn how to share life-on-life together in mission. They should comprise people committed to seeing Christ formed in one another as, by the Holy Spirit, they take the gospel and speak it as truth.

The problem with devolution on this scale is that it takes power away from the center, and many leaders struggle with that. But it is at that point that I as a leader need to hear the gospel afresh.

These people do not belong to me, but to the Lord who bought them. He is more than capable of leading them through his word and by his Spirit. Sometimes, the most delightful moments of leadership are when we see people change, even when we have had very little to do with it!

Questions for reflection

? Summarise in one sentence the end you should have in view as you lead your church.

? How do you feel about a less competent trainee taking on something you currently do? How will you deal with any resulting frustration and anxiety?

? What proportion of your time do you spend with people *with the purpose of helping them become mature in Christ?* Does that proportion need to grow? If yes, then how?

14 WHERE HAVE ALL THE GOOD MEN GONE?

Principle

Invest in leadership, particularly among men,

Consider this

Anne looked around the room, observing the people in her church with affection. She smiled as her husband passed round cups of tea and chatted with people—he was such a catch! Her eyes passed from person to person—six godly, attractive, servant-hearted single girls, two families, and a couple of single guys. The single men in their group were boys really. The question came again to her mind: *Where are all the men?*

Biblical background
Acts 2 v 1-4, 14-18; 4 v 8-20

? It wasn't long before this that the disciples were hiding away, afraid (cf. John 20 v 19). Here they speak boldly in front of the people they were afraid of. What has caused such a change in these men (2 v 4)?

? What has God promised to do (2 v 17-18)?

? What kind of men were Peter and John (4 v 13)?

? What conviction did they have as a result of being filled with the Spirit (4 v 20)?

Read all about it

It's always intrigued me that one of the perennial concerns of modern church life is conspicuous by its absence in the Bible.

Paul pursued his God-given vision of taking the gospel to the Gentiles of the ancient world. He conducted whirlwind tours preaching, planting, being persecuted and then moving on in a way we might consider completely reckless today.

Of course, he wrote letters to encourage and help the churches he planted—but here is what is missing. **He never once laments the lack of leaders.** He never mentions a shortfall in those who were prepared to step forward to take up the role of deacons, elders, shepherds.

Fast-forward 2000 years and we see a very different situation. Thousands of churches without a pastor. Theological colleges and seminaries struggling to find people who want to be trained for ministry. Local churches unable to find people to run Bible studies, Sunday-school classes or youth groups.

What has happened? Has God's Spirit deserted the churches?

This book opened with a plea for us to recognize the unhealthy influence our cultural background has on our views of leadership. I want to suggest as we close that we have so bought into a cultural view of leadership that we have failed to recognize that the Bible's view is very different, and so we fail to recognize, develop and encourage into leadership those that perfectly fit the biblical pattern.

At the same time, we have been embarrassed by the way our culture has swung away from a culturally-assumed male headship, which has distracted us from seeing the men in our congregations as the primary resource for gospel leadership in our congregations.

And the same disease has also infected our young men. In a world of sexual equality (a good thing), they have become diffident about taking up the responsibility of leadership that God has given them (a bad thing). Many young men prefer instead to remain immature, and happy to depend on others, male or female, who will step up to the role. Adolescents, become "adult-lescents".

Alpha males

Leaders that our culture praises, recognizes and aspires to are strong, articulate, entrepreneurial types. They take risks. They surge forward with innovations that break new ground and change the way the game works. They build interesting buildings. They inspire new ways of thinking.

Praise God that many of these kinds of men are active in Christian ministry. They are often the pioneering pastors who plant a church and start a new work. They are great speakers who offer new insights into God's word. They inspire people to be like them. How could we complain about that?

But hidden beneath the "success stories" of these pioneering pastors is a real problem. Because if we assume that only this kind of pastor is "the real deal", we sow the seeds that have flowered into our current problem.

As great and inspiring as these leaders are, they will often be the first to admit that *they are not the whole solution to the church leadership question*. They may be able to start something, but they are often ill equipped in their gifts and their temperament to consolidate and grow the work they have started.

I like to think of two different kinds of leader for which I do not want to apply biblical terminology. Studies have show that a disproportionate amount of people who are entrepreneurs are left handed. So let's call them *left handed* and *right handed*.

Left-handed pastors are those who are entrepreneurs. They are church planters, pioneers and go-getters. They are like Caleb, who urged the fearful Israelites to invade the promised land, and who at 85 was still up for taking a new hill from the enemy.

Right-handed pastors are no less courageous, but are able to apply themselves to consolidating, stabilizing and growing a congregation of God's people. They are more adapted to gospel ministry in the everyday routine.

Our problem is that we praise the left-handed leaders over the right-handed ones, who are just as, if not more, important! We look for those who are good "up front" in leading and public speaking, or who have creative ministry ideas, or a passion to go out and "capture a hill" for the gospel. We fail to look for those who will patiently and quietly love people, apply the gospel to their lives and their problems, and grow disciples. We have "alpha-tised" our expectations of ministry.

In chapter 3 we showed how the qualifications for ministry are really very minimal. A Christ-like life, and an aptitude to teach. Note that the aptitude is to teach—to explain carefully and clearly God's word to others. There are many ways in leadership that someone may do this without being especially good or memorable in the way they preach to larger numbers in a formal setting. Perhaps Paul never complained about a lack of leaders because he was applying different criteria to us!

He didn't put prospective candidates on a soap box in the middle of the market, and score them out of 10 for their performance. More likely, he observed them where they were in their jobs and families, and saw how they exercised leadership of the household. He marked their efforts to understand and express the gospel to others. He thought about how they showed Christ-likeness in the small details of their lives that are so often more telling in revealing our true character. How they spoke to those who were anxious. How they dealt with setbacks in their own circumstances. How they coped with criticism.

One helpful way forward might be to think about three different classes of people:

- **Potential leaders.** There are leaders all around you in your community. They may own and run a local shop or business. They may run a local sports team. They may have a thriving "business" as a drug dealer. It is not wrong to pray and work for these people to be won for the gospel. God's Spirit will transform their leadership qualities and infuse them with the character of Christ to make them valuable under-shepherds to his flock.

- **Leaders with potential.** Unrecognized in your own congregation are people who will not consider themselves leadership potential for some of the reasons outlined above. Hunt them out! Find the men whose wives speak well of them, whose children love them, who love the gospel and want to live it out, however quiet or timid they appear. Then train them biblically and theologically, mentor them, disciple them, inspire them with the idea and responsibility of Christian leadership and call them to step up to the mark.

- **Those in leadership.** There are people in many levels of leadership in your church who need to be urged to move on. I tell people: *"If you want to take this on—you've got to be prepared for me to get on your case in a way that I never would if you were not in leadership. I will get in your face, because I want you to grow and not stagnate as a leader."* Disciple them. Urge them to apply the gospel to their households, and to the issues they face in themselves and others. And remind them that even shepherds are sheep who need the care, encouragement and guidance of others.

Where have all the leaders gone? They are all around your community, waiting to hear the gospel and for God to redeem their leadership gifts for something of greater value than money or power. Pray for God to call them as you share the gospel of grace with them.

Where have all the leaders gone? They are all around your church if you have eyes to recognize them and lay before them the joyful challenge of joy of their calling in Christ

Where have all the leaders gone? They are waiting for you to invest in them so that they will no longer be happy just to "make camp" and survive this life before enjoying eternity, but will join you in leading God's people with God's word, for the glory of the One true Shepherd, Jesus Christ.

Questions for reflection

? Are you a "left-handed" or a "right-handed" leader? What do you instinctively feel about leaders of the other kind?

? How were you encouraged and developed into leadership? Whose influence was especially important? What was it they did that was so encouraging? Are you doing the same?

 Ideas for action

? Be intentional. Make a list of the people you know who fit into the three categories: potential leaders; leaders with potential; and those in leadership already. Can you write a plan for how you will encourage each person on the list?

? The Lord Jesus specifically urged us to "Ask the Lord of Harvest to send out workers into the harvest fields" (Luke 10 v 2). Are you making specific time to pray for the identification, training and deployment of new leaders?

? Pray for, and make a plan to share the gospel with some of the natural community leaders you identified who are not yet believers!

Gospel-centered marriage
becoming the couple God wants you to be

To understand why marriages struggle—as they all do—we need to understand the nature of our sin. To make marriages work, we need to understand how to apply the truth about God and His salvation. This study guide on Christian marriage focuses on how the gospel shapes the practical realities of everyday life. Tim Chester lifts the lid on many of the common pressure points, and shows how a proper understanding of the gospel can shape a response.

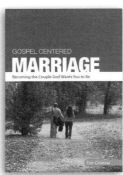

Gospel-centered family
becoming the parents God wants you to be

Many books aim to raise up competent, balanced parents and well-trained, well-rounded children. But Tim Chester and Ed Moll focus on families growing God-knowing, Christ-confessing, grace-receiving, servant-hearted, mission-minded believers—adults and children together. In twelve concise chapters, this book challenges us to become the distinctively different people that God, through His gospel, calls us to be.

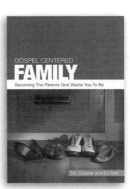

FOR MORE INFORMATION AND TO ORDER:
UK and Europe: www.thegoodbook.co.uk
North America: www.thegoodbook.com
Australia: www.thegoodbook.com.au
New Zealand: www.thegoodbook.co.nz

Gospel-centered church
becoming the community God wants you to be

In *Gospel-centered church*, Steve Timmis and Tim Chester explain that gospel ministry is much more than simply evangelism. It is about shaping the whole of our church life and activities by the content and imperatives of the gospel. It is about ensuring that our church or group is motivated by and focused on the gospel, as opposed to our traditions. This workbook is designed to help clarify our thinking about how we should live our lives as the people of God.

Gospel-centered life
becoming the person God wants you to be

How can ordinary Christians live the truly extraordinary life that God calls us to? By focusing our attention on the grace of God shown to us in the gospel, everyday problems familiar to Christians everywhere can be transformed as the cross of Christ becomes the motive and measure of everything we do. *Gospel-centered life* shows how every Christian can follow the way of the cross, as they embrace the liberating grace of God.

FOR MORE INFORMATION AND TO ORDER:
UK and Europe: www.thegoodbook.co.uk
North America: www.thegoodbook.com
Australia: www.thegoodbook.com.au
New Zealand: www.thegoodbook.co.nz

Covers may vary from those shown.

thegoodbook
COMPANY

At The Good Book Company, we are dedicated to helping Christians and local churches grow. We believe that God's growth process always starts with hearing clearly what He has said to us through his timeless word—the Bible.

Ever since we opened our doors in 1991, we have been striving to produce resources that honor God in the way the Bible is used. We have grown to become an international provider of user-friendly resources to the Christian community, with believers of all backgrounds and denominations using our Bible studies, books, evangelistic resources, DVD-based courses and training events.

We want to equip ordinary Christians to live for Christ day by day, and churches to grow in their knowledge of God, their love for one another, and the effectiveness of their outreach.

Call us for a discussion of your needs or visit one of our local websites for more information on the resources and services we provide.

North America: www.thegoodbook.com
UK & Europe: www.thegoodbook.co.uk
Australia: www.thegoodbook.com.au
New Zealand: www.thegoodbook.co.nz

North America: 866 244 2165
UK & Europe: 0333 123 0880
Australia: (02) 6100 4211
New Zealand (+64) 3 343 1990

www.christianityexplored.org
Our partner site is a great place for those exploring the Christian faith, with a clear explanation of the gospel, powerful testimonies and answers to difficult questions.

One life. What's it all about?